D1206038

Turn-Taking, Fingerspelling, and Contact in Signed Languages

Ceil Lucas, General Editor

Turn-Taking, Fingerspelling, and Contact

in Signed Languages

Ceil Lucas, Editor

GALLAUDET UNIVERSITY PRESS

Washington, D.C.

Sociolinguistics in Deaf Communities
A Series Edited by Ceil Lucas

Gallaudet University Press
Washington, D.C. 20002

ISBN 1-56368-128-5
ISSN 1080-5494

Contents

Editorial Advisory Board

Contributors

Delfina Aliaga-Emetrio
Casal Deaf Association
Barcelona, Spain

Jesús Amador Alonso-Rodríguez
Deaf Association of Sabadell
Sabadell, Spain

Rosa María Boldú-Menasanch
Center for the Teaching of LSC
Barcelona, Spain

Paul Dudis
Department of Linguistics
University of California,
   Berkeley

Júlia Garrusta-Ribes
University of Barcelona
Barcelona, Spain

Victòria Gras-Ferrer
University of Barcelona
Barcelona, Spain

Mieke Van Herreweghe
English Department
Ghent University
Flanders, Belgium

Esperanza Morales-López
Universidade da Coruña
Coruña, Spain

Kristin J. Mulrooney
Department of Linguistics and
   Interpretation
Gallaudet University
Washington, D.C.

Bruce A. Sofinski
American Sign Language
   Program
University of Virginia
Charlottesville, Virginia

Introduction

Volume 8 of the Sociolinguistics in Deaf Communities series continues the tradition of the series with a collection of papers ranging in topics from variation in fingerspelling and the outcomes of ASL-English contact to the structure of sign language discourse, turn-taking strategies, and language attitudes. With studies in this volume from the United States, Belgium, and Spain, the series continues to show us the wide range of sociolinguistic issues that arise in Deaf communities around the world. It is my hope that the studies in this volume and, indeed, in this whole series will provide a useful resource for researchers, practitioners, and community members.

I am grateful to the contributors to this volume and to the members of the editorial advisory board for their work in putting this book together. I also gratefully acknowledge Ivey Pittle Wallace, the assistant editorial director, Deirdre Mullervy, managing editor, and Mary Gawlik, copy editor, at Gallaudet University Press for their support, hard work, and good humor.

Turn-Taking, Fingerspelling, and Contact in Signed Languages

Part I Variation

Variation in ASL Fingerspelling

Kristin J. Mulrooney

Students enrolled in American Sign Language (ASL) interpreter preparation programs often comment that male signers and female signers sign "differently." These students may not be able to articulate the technical differences in production but will make statements such as "Women signers are easier to understand." The goal of this study is to compare signing by males and females by focusing on their fingerspelling production and thereby determine whether a difference exists in how men and women produce fingerspelled signs. My hypothesis is that male signers use more noncitation-form fingerspelled signs, which are more difficult to perceive. Citation form can be defined as the unmarked version of a sign. If one were to look up a sign in an ASL dictionary, the sign would be shown with a picture of this version. The unmarked version of a sign is similar to the standard pronunciation of a word in spoken languages if a standard pronunciation indeed exists. A citation form for fingerspelling is the form one would expect if a signer were to carefully articulate the sign. It is also the form most likely to be taught in ASL classes. Noncitation form would be any variation of the citation form. This variation may be produced by a change in handshape, in orientation, or in location of the sign's production. A word that is fingerspelled with individual, noncitation-form letters is difficult to comprehend, which may be a factor in interpreter students stating that male signers are more difficult to understand than female signers.

This chapter is the culmination of work on my guided research project; however, it has been supported, influenced, shaped, enhanced, and polished by many hands besides my own. I would therefore like to extend my deepest appreciation to the many individuals who contributed to its development. They include Robert Bayley, University of Texas San Antonio; Natalie Schilling-Estes, Georgetown University; Ron Reed, Gallaudet University Television Department; and Neil Schaefer, Gallaudet University. I appreciate the feedback from the two reviewers; the chapter has been strengthened because of their insights: James Rhilinger for his unwavering support and, most importantly, Ceil Lucas because without her guidance, patience, and seemingly endless insights, I would never have completed this project.

3

ASL Fingerspelling

In studies of ASL, fingerspelling is often overlooked. Few researchers have studied this component of the language. This lack of research can be largely attributed to the misconception that fingerspelling is not a true feature of ASL. Historically, fingerspelling has been perceived as a manual representation of English. Klima and Bellugi (1979), in their efforts to describe how signs in ASL are formed, discounted fingerspelling as a possible avenue for offering insight into the structure of signs. They remark, "But fingerspelling is a derived, secondary gestural system, based on English. Our interest is in the internal organization of the signs of a primary gestural system." Thus, fingerspelling was set aside as not an integral part of ASL.

Fingerspelling might have continued to be ignored in ASL research had the field not changed its perception of how signs were formed. In 1989, Liddell and Johnson published their research titled "American Sign Language: The Phonological Base." This work challenged the belief that the parts of signs were simultaneously produced. Until this point, linguists studying ASL followed the Stokoe system (Stokoe, Casterline, and Croneberg 1965). This system proposed that ASL was structurally different from spoken languages. In spoken languages, a bundle of articulatory features combine to produce a sound. By itself, this sound, has no meaning. When a group of sounds are strung together in a particular way, they can form a word that is meaningful in a given language. Stokoe believed that signs had three parts (tabula, designator, and signation), which combined simultaneously to make a sign. This idea of simultaneous production was vastly different from spoken languages, which produced meaningful words by sequentially combining sounds that had been formed from articulatory bundles. Liddell and Johnson (1989) showed that ASL signs are in fact formed sequentially and that the phonology of sign languages is like that of spoken languages.

The basic premise of the Liddell and Johnson system is that signs consist of hold segments (H) and movement segments (M) that are produced sequentially. Holds are defined as periods of time during which all aspects of an articulation bundle are in a steady state. Movements are defined as periods of time during which some aspect of articulation is in transition. Movement and holds would be equivalent to consonants and vowels in spoken languages. Within any hold or movement is information about the handshape, location, orientation, and nonmanual signals, which when combined, forms bundles of articulatory features. What this new perspective allows is a more accurate description of signs that allows their components to be analyzed. It also shows that fingerspelling is in fact a core part of the language. A fingerspelled sign is formed using the same phonological rules that created other signs. Each letter is composed of a segment (or more in the case of J and Z) having a handshape, an orientation, and a location. The fact that twenty-four of the letters use only a hold is unimportant because other ASL signs also have this structure, for example, the sign COLOR. The letters J and Z have structures of H-M-H and H-M-H-M-H-M-H respectively. Many signs also have this kind of structure, for example, the signs GOOD and YEAR. Through analyzing ASL fingerspelling signs, we can gain insight into the language itself.

Despite this information, many people continue to hesitate in accepting fingerspelling as ASL signs. It is true that the handshapes of fingerspelled signs often resemble the written symbol. For example, the fingerspelled sign for *c,* looks the written letter *c.* Other letters look nothing like the letters they represent. For instance, the fingerspelled sign for *s,* looks nothing like its written counterpart (see p. 13). These signs may have developed as a direct result of language contact with English, but they are signs and not letters. If a native user of ASL fingerspelled a word to a native user of English (who was unfamiliar with ASL), the English user would have no idea what the string of fingerspelled signs meant.

Also important to note is that users of ASL use fingerspelling frequently in everyday conversation. A signer will switch back and forth regularly from signs to fingerspelling. Padden (1991) reports that fingerspelled words frequently make up 7–10 percent of the overall vocabulary in everyday signing. In the data collected for this study, an average of twelve fingerspelled words were used during a two-minute segment of discourse. Fingerspelling is not a marked event in ASL because fingerspelled signs are simply signs like any other. In contrast, if a person using spoken English spelled twelve words during two minutes of discourse, a native English listener would certainly notice. The listener would probably look around to see whether any children were present who were not supposed to understand what was being discussed. Fingerspelling is used in ASL precisely because it is a component of the language, which does not preclude fingerspelling being used in other contexts in which it is attended to more carefully by a signer. For instance, when a person is being introduced, the signer may point with his or her weak hand toward the hand that is fingerspelling the name to bring the listener's eye gaze toward the hand (Davis 1989).

Other researchers have analyzed fingerspelling in ASL, and their studies have contributed to our understanding of how it is used by native users. Akamatsu (1982) and Hanson (1981) analyzed how ASL users comprehend fingerspelled words when individual fingerspelled letters may be incompletely articulated or omitted. Both Wilcox (1992) and Brentari (1998) address the phonetics of ASL fingerspelling in their works. How fingerspelling is acquired by deaf children is addressed by both Padden (1991) and Blumenthal-Kelly (1995). Blumenthal-Kelly (1991) also analyzed fingerspelling use among Deaf senior citizens. The current study benefits from the research that preceded it and attempts to contribute further by focusing on variation in fingerspelling and by determining what factors may contribute to this variation.

Lexicalized Fingerspelling

Ten years before the publication of Liddell and Johnson's (1989) work on ASL phonology, another ASL linguist was conducting the first research on fingerspelling in ASL. Robbin Battison (1978) noticed that English words that were fingerspelled often changed in their production over time. Suppose a signer wanted to represent the English word *job* using fingerspelling. The signer would produce each sign (a free morpheme) distinctly; this process is called full fingerspelling and is represented with dashes: J-O-B. Battison observed that some of these separate morphemes that occurred frequently in ASL discourse began to act like a single morpheme, like a single sign. This activity is referred to as lexicalized fingerspelling, and the symbol # is used in front of the letters to mark it. Returning to our example, J-O-B became lexicalized because the production of the individual morphemes changed. When #JOB is signed, one sees the beginning of a J morpheme, the elimination of the O morpheme, and a change in the orientation of the B morpheme. Battison explained that fingerspelled signs undergo pressure to conform to the rules of ASL structure. One of these rules is that no more than two handshapes are allowed in a sign. Eliminating the O handshape in J-O-B allows for this rule to be followed. Note that exceptions to this rule do occur, however; for example, the lexicalized sign #EARLY has three handshapes.

Variation in ASL—Gender Differences

Studies of language variation between men and women have shown that women tend to favor the standard pronunciation of words whereas men are more likely to use nonstandard forms. Trudgill (1972) showed that marked differences occur between the word usage of working-class males and that of working-class females. Males favored pronunciations such as singin' rather than singing. In his analysis, Trudgill suggested a number of reasons for these differences. Women, who are perhaps more insecure in their social position and therefore more status conscious than men, may use standard forms of the language to signal their status in society. The nonstandard language that men more frequently used was perceived as masculine, and women disassociated themselves from this form by using speech that was regarded as more refined. Another study in Reading, England, by Cheshire (1978) found that lower-class boys use more nonstandard syntax than lower-class girls do. The study suggested that the boys used the nonstandard syntax to show solidarity and resist the use of Standard English. Labov (1981) expands on this topic by stating that, if linguistic usage is stratified by style and class, then one can expect differences between men and women. In these situations, women will show preference for forms that have more prestige in society. However, he adds the following corollary: "It is important to bear in mind that this shift of women toward higher prestige forms . . . is limited to those societies where women play a role in public life." Labov believes that, in a society in which status can be changed, women will use the preferred standard forms to gain higher status.

Labov's assertion is interesting when placed in the context of American Sign Language, a minority language in the greater American society. In addition, a number of studies point to gender differences in ASL signing. The first was by Nowell (1989) in which she looked at conversational differences between men and women. The total amount of talk as well as the use of questions and feedback were used as measures for these differences as has been done in similar studies of spoken languages. The analysis revealed little difference between men and women in these three areas. The data for this study were limited to twelve participants, and the subjects were interviewed to elicit signing samples, which did not reflect a casual conversation experience. In addition, one of the interviewers was a hearing researcher, which also may have altered the results.

McMurtrie (1993) looked at gender differences in the use of feedback in ASL conversations. This study resulted in the same conclusions as

Nowell's (1989): Little difference occurred between the amount or type of feedback given by men and that given by women. McMurtrie's study involved only four deaf adults, two men and two women, and the total amount of videotape analyzed is never disclosed, which makes it difficult to generalize the results to the larger Deaf community.

Lexical differences in male and female ASL users have also been researched. In Mansfield (1993), five subjects were asked to show the interviewer a sign for thirty-one stimulus pictures. The results suggested that lexical variations relating to specific content area did exist, but not at great enough levels to assert a male-only or female-only associated lexicon. Mansfield did note the occurrence of phonological variations—specifically, that women used fingerspelling more frequently than males.

In the area of ASL discourse, Malloy and Donner (1995) examined whether ASL narratives paralleled what was found in spoken language narratives. They discovered that men used reiteration more frequently than women, which was the opposite for spoken language narratives. Unfortunately, only two native ASL users were videotaped telling a story; therefore, generalization to all ASL users cannot be made confidently. In addition, the narratives were not stories made up by the subjects. They were asked to tell the story from the children's book *The Snowman*. This factor also may have influenced the stories that were produced.

More recently, Wulf's (1998) study of gender differences in ASL signers focused on phonological differences. Wulf videotaped and analyzed nine Deaf native ASL signers and one nonnative signer and clearly demonstrated a difference between men and women in the lower boundary of signing space. Men consistently ended their production of a sign at a lower space than female signers. As in all the studies, a limited number of subjects were analyzed, and they were all from a rather homogeneous population (Gallaudet University students).

These studies open up the discussion about gender differences in ASL, and all raise interesting and worthwhile questions for understanding variation in ASL. They also point to the need to analyze a comprehensive corpus of data to allow broader generalization to ASL users. Of the five studies reviewed here, Wulf's is the most useful in laying the groundwork for analyzing phonological differences in ASL. Her analysis has pinpointed a significant production difference that may be the basis for other phonological variations.

Variation in ASL—Fingerspelling

Phonological differences in fingerspelling between male and female signers may help account for the complaint often made by sign language interpreters that it is easier to understand female signers than male signers. The specific difficulty most often cited in connection with comprehending male ASL signers is that men's fingerspelling is much harder to understand. The question is why?

The original goal of this study was to compare fingerspelling by males and females and determine whether a difference exists in how men and women produce fingerspelled signs. The process of asking this question revealed additional insight with respect to what contributed to variation in fingerspelling: The grammatical function of the word being fingerspelled influenced whether citation- or noncitation-form letters were used.

The present study was preceded by a pilot study that used a small number of examples. The pilot study proved invaluable because it highlighted some flaws in the data-coding methods that were used and emphasized the need to expand the number of tokens (one token equals one fingerspelled sign) in this study.

The following sections describe the data that were used for both the pilot and final study. First, the pilot study and its results are presented, including the problems that arose and how they were addressed in the final study. Next follows a description of the final study, including the study's results.

THE DATA

Research on ASL has proven challenging for a number of reasons. Most prominent is the difficulty researchers encounter when trying to record ASL in use. Spoken language researchers grapple with the Observer's Paradox: "Any systematic observation of speech defines a context in which some conscious attention will be paid to that speech, so it will be difficult, without great ingenuity, to observe the genuine 'vernacular'" (Labov 1972, 61). This paradox explains how difficult it is to obtain "natural" speech from informants because the act of recording informants' speech often influences what is produced and causes "unnatural" speech.

In sign language research, this problem can be exacerbated in two ways. First, a videotape camera is the instrument used to record sign languages. This tool for data collection is much more obtrusive than a tape recorder. It takes longer to set up, one has to make sure it has been properly focused and adjusted for the signing space, and there is the nagging feeling every informant feels that there is an '"eye" staring directly at them. The fact that the informant's identity cannot be concealed enhances these problems. With voices, identity is easier to mask. Often, voices sound slightly different on tape compared with those same voices in real life. People listening to an audiotape likely would not recognize the person whose voice they heard on the tape if they met this person on the street. This luxury is not afforded to the person who is videotaped.

The second issue is one only hearing (not Deaf) ASL researchers confront. The fact that a researcher can hear will dramatically affect the way a native Deaf ASL user will sign. Lucas and Valli (1992) showed that native ASL users will sign using less ASL grammar and much more English-like structure when signing to a hearing ASL user rather than a Deaf ASL user. Attempts to avoid these difficulties influenced the selection of data material used for analysis in this study.

To reduce the effect of these issues, the data used were rough footage recorded by producers of a television series called "Deaf Mosaic," produced by the Gallaudet University Television Department. This series was aired over a ten-year period, from the early 1980s until the early 1990s. The program featured a variety of successful Deaf people around the United States and the world. A Deaf interviewer would interview the featured person for about an hour. In addition to this interview, cameras typically followed the featured person to record whatever activity the program intended to document. The idea at the inception of this study was to use as data the footage that was made as the person was followed. These data had the potential to be more natural because they would be informal, and the person likely would become engaged in the activity being performed and be less conscious of the video camera. Unfortunately, a number of events arose to prevent these data from being used. Foremost among them was that many of the informal situations that were on the videotape did not allow for accurate analysis. For instance, the camera was too far away to clearly record fingerspelling or the person signing had his or her back to the camera, which made it impossible to see what was being said. Despite this setback, the footage recorded in the formal interview portions of the videotapes proved very useful as data.

The data used had a number of advantages. First, the data were collected by Deaf people. Therefore, the phenomenon identified by Lucas and Valli (1992) in which Deaf informants alter their signing style was minimized. Second, a professional television crew collected these data. They have expertise in how to videotape, including where best to position a camera so viewing the person who is signing is easiest. Also, the quality of the videotape was much higher than the quality of tapes recorded by amateur photographers. The high quality proved tremendously important in the analysis stage, allowing clear images of the handshapes being used. Finally, another advantage of these data was that they matched the focus of this particular study. This study was not concerned with obtaining pure ASL. The focus was on the phonology of the signs, not the syntax. The data were not affected by a signer who might use more English-like signing because he or she was nervous or conscious of the filming. The study was concerned with the formation of individual fingerspelled signs and not with where these occurred in the sentence.

The data comprised eight interviews with deaf subjects, four males and four females. The individuals discussed vastly different topics: body-building, furniture refinishing, adoption, farming, skydiving, and theater. Despite the variation in topics, all subjects used fingerspelling throughout the interviews. Four of the subjects were middle aged (thirty-five-forty-five years old), two were in their late sixties, one subject was in her mid-twenties, and one was in his late fifties. All ages are approximations based on information stated in the interviews (what year a piece of land was purchased, for example). The subjects included three married couples and two single people. All interviews were conducted in a similar fashion. The interviewer asked the subject to impart a bit of biographical information and then asked questions related to the specific topic being discussed.

THE PILOT STUDY

The pilot study was the first attempt to determine the constraints on the variability of fingerspelling. The factors recorded in the coding are those features that the author initially believed might contribute to the variation found in fingerspelling.

Coding—Pilot Study

The interviews were watched, and the following information was collected:

- What the fingerspelled word was
- The time on the videotape that it occurred

- Whether this fingerspelled word was a lexicalized word or non-lexicalized word
- The function of the word (noun, verb, adjective)
- The individual fingerspelled sign (the "letter")
- The articulatory features of the fingerspelled sign (handshape, location, and orientation)[1]
- Whether the individual fingerspelled sign was produced in citation form (+CF) or noncitation form (−CF)
- What preceded the fingerspelled sign (fingerspelling, sign, or pause)
- What followed the fingerspelled sign (fingerspelling, sign, or pause)

This study distinguishes between a fingerspelled sign and fingerspelled word. The former refers to the individual "letter," and the latter refers to a string of fingerspelled signs that form a word. The fingerspelled word B-U-S is made from three fingerspelled signs.

Central to this study is whether the signer produced noncitation forms or citation forms of the fingerspelled signs. As stated in the introduction, citation form can be defined as the unmarked version of a sign. If one were to look up a sign in an ASL dictionary, he or she would find a picture of this version. The unmarked version of a sign is similar in spoken languages to the standard pronunciation of a word if in fact this standard exists. A citation form for fingerspelling is the form one would expect if a signer were carefully articulating the sign. It is also the form most likely to be taught in ASL classes. Noncitation form would be any variation away from citation form. Therefore, when looking at each individual fingerspelled sign, a judgment was made as to whether it was representative of citation form or noncitation form. To illustrate, the citation form of the finger-spelled sign K would look like figure 1. If a signer extended the thumb rather than have it in contact with the middle finger, it would be considered noncitation form. This noncitation articulation of the fingerspelled sign may resemble the numeral 3.

Any given word could be composed of any combination of + or − citation forms. A word may be carefully articulated, with each fingerspelled sign being produced using its citation form. A word may include a combination of citation-form and noncitation-form fingerspelled signs; for

1. The Liddell and Johnson (1989) notation system was used because this system allows for the most accurate description of signs.

FIGURE 1. *The C, K, and S handshapes*

example, the first and last fingerspelled signs may be citation form and the intervening fingerspelled signs, noncitation form. I believe that noncitation-form fingerspelled signs are more difficult for nonnative signers to identify and, therefore, that comprehension of the entire fingerspelled word is more difficult.

The study's hypothesis is that male signers use noncitation-form fingerspelled signs more often than female signers. The pilot study was used to flesh out what other factors influence whether citation or noncitation forms of fingerspelling were used.

The VARBRUL program was used to analyze the data. VARBRUL is a computerized tool to aid in the analysis of linguistic variation and was developed by Henrietta Cedergren and David Sankoff (1974). Variable rule analysis assumes that a linguistic phenomenon with two possible alternatives exists. In this study, these alternatives would be the use of citation- or noncitation-form fingerspelling. The variable rule metaphor assumes that there are "applications" and "nonapplications" of a "rule." Variable rule analysis assumes that various factors influence which of the two alternatives (citation or noncitation form) will be realized. These factors do not guarantee one or the other alternative but will simply increase or decrease the likelihood of a rule application. A numerical measure of each factor's influence is calculated. The values range between 0 and 1. A factor with a weighting greater than 0.500 is said to favor the application of the rule being examined. Factors with values less than 0.500 are said to disfavor the rule, and factors with values at 0.500 are said to have no effect.

Factor groups had to be established before VARBRUL could be used. After the data were coded, I identified five factors as playing a possible role in the variation. The factor groups identified in the pilot study were gender (male or female), lexicalization (lexicalized or nonlexicalized), orientation (prone or neutral), preceding sign (fingerspelling, sign, or pause), and following sign (fingerspelling, sign, or pause).

An explanation about the factor groups of preceding sign and following sign as well as what those groups were attempting to capture may be useful. Each fingerspelled sign represented one token. The fingerspelled word C-A-T has three fingerspelled signs, or three tokens. Other signs were not counted as tokens; however, they could potentially affect the production of a token, especially if they come directly before or after it. For instance, in a sequence such as TOMORROW J-O-H-N LEAVE that includes a fingerspelled word, the fingerspelled sign J would be preceded by the sign TOMORROW and followed by the fingerspelled sign O. The fingerspelled sign O would be preceded and followed by fingerspelled signs J and H respectively. A pause indicates that no signing occurred; for example, a pause might occur before the first word in a sentence.

Another point of clarification has to do with the orientation factor group. In the Liddell and Johnson (1989) notation system, orientation actually can be described in four ways: prone, supine, super-prone, and neutral. The analysis portion of the pilot study found that, with a single exception, all fingerspelled signs used either the prone or neutral position. This finding makes intuitive sense because prone (palm facing outward) and neutral (palm facing to the side) positions are the easiest to produce and see.

Once the factor groups were established, I developed a grid to account for all the possible combinations of these factors, a total of 72 possible combinations. I returned to the coded data and tabulated for each of the possibilities how many citation and noncitation forms were produced. Noncitation form was considered application of the feature, and citation form was nonapplication of the feature. Among my data, only 31 of the possible 72 combinations produced instances of fingerspelled signs.

These numbers were then entered into the VARBRUL program and the program was run. For the men, 39 words had been coded, yielding a total of 154 tokens. For the women, 39 words had been coded for a total of 158 tokens. This total of 312 tokens is considered a very small number for the VARBRUL program.

Results—Pilot Study

The VARBRUL analysis highlighted that certain factors do favor the use of the noncitation form (see table 1). Most significant, a fingerspelled sign with neutral orientation favored the production of a noncitation form of the fingerspelled sign (.66). The next most influential factor was what preceded the fingerspelled sign. If another fingerspelled sign preceded the fingerspelled sign in question, this would favor the production of a noncitation-form fingerspelled sign (.54). The noncitation form of the fingerspelled sign (−CF) was also favored if the preceding sign was a pause (.51). The following sign also had an influence albeit less so. If the following sign was another sign, it favored −CF (.52). Finally, if the signer was a male, this favored the production of −CF (.52) compared with females who disfavored −CF (.48).

A second part to the VARBRUL analysis is the step-up and step-down procedure. This procedure tests all of the factor groups for significance, first by adding them one at a time to the analysis (step-up) and then by subtracting them one at a time (step-down). Each time something is added, it is testing whether the inclusion of a given factor group on the analysis produces a statistically significant improvement in the fit between the estimated probabilities and the observed data. In the step-up and step-down analysis, some discrepancy seems to occur with respect to which factor groups are significant. In the step-up, the program appears to throw out the gender factor group and the lexicalization factor group. In the step-down analysis, the program appears to throw out lexicalized, orientation, and preceding factor groups. This analysis left following sign as the only remaining factor group.

TABLE 1. *Results of Binomial Variable Rule Analysis (Application value: −CF)*

Factor Group		Weighting
Gender	Male	.52
	Female	.48
Lexicalization	Lexicalized	.46
	Non-Lexicalized	.51
Orientation	Prone	.45
	Neutral	.66
Preceding	Fingerspelling	.54
	Sign	.31
	Pause	.51
Following	Fingerspelling	.50
	Sign	.52
	Pause	.35

Discussion—Pilot Study

The results of the VARBRUL run were perplexing. In the step-up run, the analysis suggests eliminating the gender factor group, which means it is not significant in contributing to whether or not a citation-form finger-spelled sign is made. This finding would mean that my hypothesis was incorrect. In addition, the program identified orientation, lexicalization, and preceding sign to be eliminated as factor groups. This finding would have left me with a single factor group, that of following sign.

The discrepancy showed that I needed to reassess the factor groups that I was using and determine whether I needed to include others. My reassessment revealed that orientation was not a factor that would influence whether a fingerspelled sign was citation or noncitation form; it was a description of what the actual fingerspelled sign looked like if it was citation or noncitation form. I decided to eliminate that factor group.

I then thought about what I was trying to capture with the preceding sign and following sign factor groups. What I wanted to know was where these preceding and following signs were being signed and whether or not this location was influencing the production of fingerspelled signs. One way of evaluating whether or not a fingerspelled sign was a noncitation form was to determine whether or not it was produced in the area near the shoulder of the dominant hand, where fingerspelling is most typically produced (see figure 2). Perhaps, then, if the sign occurring immediately before or after the fingerspelled sign in question happened in this area, the fingerspelled sign would more likely be produced as a citation form.

I decided to retain both the gender factor group and lexicalized factor group because of the original belief that gender may be contributing to the variation. I was hoping the reason gender was being thrown out during the step-up run of VARBRUL was because I had such few tokens, a total of 312.

I decided to include one other factor group, that of grammatical function. I had coded for this function in the pilot study but did not use it as a factor group. Five other studies on ASL variation (Lucas 1995; Hoopes 1998; Bayley, Lucas, and Rose 2000; Lucas, Bayley, Rose, and Wulf forthcoming; Lucas, Bayley, and Valli 2001) found that grammatical function can be the strongest constraint on variation. Following the lead of these studies, I decided to incorporate grammatical function as a factor group.

In summary, the effort to reassess the factor groups led to eliminating the orientation factor group, emphasizing location within the preceding

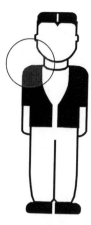

FIGURE 2. The area on the body where fingerspelling is most often produced

sign and following sign factor groups, and adding a grammatical function factor group. After making these changes, I coded the data again.

THE FINAL STUDY

The data were coded the second time in the same manner as the pilot study. The following information was recorded:

- What the fingerspelled word was
- The time on the videotape that it occurred
- Whether this fingerspelled word was a lexicalized word or non-lexicalized word
- The function of the word (noun, verb, adjective)
- The individual fingerspelled sign (the letter)
- Whether the individual fingerspelled sign was produced in citation form (+CF) or noncitation form (−CF)
- Where the preceding the sign, if there was a sign, was produced (fingerspelling location, nonfingerspelling location, or pause)
- Where the preceding the sign, if there was a sign, was produced (fingerspelling location, nonfingerspelling location, or pause)

This information included the five factor groups that would be used. The first factor group determined what the word's grammatical function was in the sentence. This factor group was divided into three options:

proper noun, noun, or verb. Included with verbs were adverbs and adjectives because too few examples of these occurred to warrant a separate group. The second factor group determined whether or not the preceding sign was produced in the traditional fingerspelling area or whether it was preceded by a pause. Likewise, the third factor group determined whether or not the following sign was produced in the traditional fingerspelling area or whether it was followed by a pause. Considering the second and third factor groups, for example, if the excerpt being transcribed were SAME K-I-T-C-H-E-N HAVE, then K would be preceded by a sign that occurred outside the traditional fingerspelling area but would be followed by I, which in this instance, occurred in the traditional fingerspelled area. The fourth factor group determined gender. The fifth factor group determined whether the fingerspelled word was a lexicalized or nonlexicalized word.

Two additional signers were added to the original six. The total number of tokens was also increased from 312 to 1,327. The coded data were entered into GoldVarb 2.1, a Macintosh version of the VARBRUL program described for the pilot project, and a VARBRUL run was performed on the data. Each signer was assigned a code to allow individual differences to be identified.

Results—Final Study

The VARBRUL analysis highlighted which factors contribute to the production of citation- or noncitation-form fingerspelling (see table 2). In neither the step-up nor step-down analysis were any factor groups thrown out by VARBRUL. The most unexpected result from the VARBRUL run was that the grammatical function (noun, proper noun, or verb) of the word being fingerspelled had the most significant influence on whether or not a citation or noncitation fingerspelled sign was produced. As table 2 shows, proper nouns favor (0.615) the production of a citation form sign. This finding makes intuitive sense because these are primarily people's names or the name of a specific place that the speaker wants to make clear to the listener. The results show that nouns slightly disfavor (0.494) the use of citation form; however, this result is almost neutral. Finally, verbs strongly disfavor (0.420) the use of citation form fingerspelled signs.

Results for the next factor group listed in the table 2 (following sign) show that instances in which the sign following the sign in question is in the traditional fingerspelled area or in which no sign follows the sign in question (pause) seem to have little influence on whether the sign in ques-

TABLE 2. *Results of Binomial Variable Rule Analysis (Application value: +CF)*

Factor Group	Weighting	Total Number	Number of Nonapplication	Percentage of Nonapplication	Number of Application	Percentage of Application
Grammatical function						
Verb	0.420	374	133	36%	241	64%
Noun	0.494	660	286	43%	374	57%
Proper noun	0.615	293	179	61%	114	39%
Following sign						
Nonfingerspelled area	0.328	302	83	27%	219	79%
Pause	0.492	37	15	41%	22	59%
Fingerspelled area	0.555	988	500	51%	488	49%
Gender						
Male	0.416	618	228	37%	390	63%
Female	0.573	709	370	52%	339	48%
Lexicalization						
Nonlexicalized	0.334	1136	552	49%	584	51%
Lexicalized	0.529	191	46	26%	145	76%

Note: CHI-square = 1.97; LOG likelihood = −843.54.

tion uses citation or noncitation form (0.555 and 0.492, respectively). However, instances in which a fingerspelled sign is followed by a sign that is outside the traditional fingerspelled area strongly disfavor the use of the citation form in the fingerspelled sign.

Results of the analysis for the gender factor group appear to show that whether the signer is a male or a female does in fact influence the signer's tendency to favor citation or noncitation forms. Males disfavor (0.416) the use of citation form fingerspelled signs whereas females favored (0.573) the use of citation form fingerspelled signs.

Finally, analysis shows that, when the fingerspelled word is lexicalized, the fingerspelled signs composing it will slightly disfavor (0.529) citation form and, when the fingerspelled word is nonlexicalized, the fingerspelled signs composing it will favor (0.334) citation form.

Discussion—Final Study

What can be gleaned from the results of this VARBRUL analysis? To begin, the grammatical function of the word being fingerspelled clearly influences how the fingerspelled sign is produced. This result was unanticipated and, as outlined in the introduction, not the intended focus of this study. The fact that verbs disfavor citation form may not be surprising if one believes that verbs are more likely to become lexicalized. Signs such as #FIX and #BACK may be cited as common examples. After reviewing the data, however, other nonlexicalized verbs also used noncitation form fingerspelled signs, including, for instance, HARVEST, DIP, ADJUST, PLOW, and DROP. Results in this study, like results in previous studies (Lucas, Bayley, and Valli 2001), suggest that grammatical function is a consistent factor in explaining variation. This finding may be counterintuitive because one would expect that phonological factors would be contributing to the variation; however, repeatedly in ASL, grammatical function appears to contribute to variation.

This study also points to the fact that lexicalized words do not necessitate the use of noncitation-form fingerspelled signs. Although the tendency for noncitation forms to occur is strong, variations can be found. For example, one subject signed #OK, producing a citation form O and citation form K, and another subject signed #TOY, producing all the fingerspelled signs in citation form. Conversely, nonlexicalized fingerspelled words are not always produced using citation-form fingerspelled signs.

Finally, this study provides some evidence to justify what students enrolled in interpreter training programs believe—that men and women fingerspell differently. Perhaps, because male signers favor the use of noncitation-form fingerspelled signs, nonnative users of ASL have more difficulty comprehending the entire fingerspelled word. If, for instance, a five-letter word is fingerspelled and three of the fingerspelled signs are noncitation form, then one may have difficulty determining what the complete word is. Even if the first and final letter are clear, without the intervening three letters, a person may still not be able to discern what word is being spelled.

CONCLUSION

The results of this study show clear tendencies in ASL as to the use of citation form fingerspelled letters; however, it is necessary to qualify that this study was a small one, with only eight subjects. In addition, these results should be considered as preliminary in that additional data are needed across a range of natural settings and registers. Although the subjects were from various parts of the country and of various ages, these other social factors were not captured by this study, and they may have been useful in articulating other influences on fingerspelling. Additional studies that expand the number of subjects in each social factor group (age, region, ethnic background, socioeconomic status) would be useful to elicit a clearer understanding as to what influences variation in fingerspelling in ASL.

Clearly, a number of factors influence when citation- and noncitation-form fingerspelled signs are being produced in ASL discourse. Counter to intuition, the grammatical function of the word appears to have slightly more influence than the phonological factors. ASL appears to parallel spoken languages in that males tend to favor the use of noncitation-form letters.

REFERENCES

Akamatsu, C. 1982. The acquisition of fingerspelling in pre-school children. Ph.D. dissertation, University of Rochester, New York.
Battison, R. 1978. *Lexical borrowing in American Sign Language.* Silver Spring, Md.: Linstok Press.
Bayley, R., C. Lucas, and M. Rose. 2000. Variation in American Sign Language: The case of DEAF. *Journal of Sociolinguistics* 4(1):81–107.

Blumenthal-Kelly, A. 1991. Fingerspelling use among the deaf senior citizens of Baltimore. In *Communication Forum*, ed. E. Winston, vol. 1, 90–98. Washington, D.C.: School of Communication, Gallaudet University.

———. 1995. Fingerspelling interaction: A set of Deaf parents and their daughter. In *Sociolinguistics in Deaf Communities*, ed. C. Lucas, 62–73. Sociolinguistics in Deaf Communities series, vol. 1. Washington, D.C.: Gallaudet University Press.

Brentari, D. 1998. *A prosodic model of sign language phonology.* Cambridge, Mass.: MIT Press.

Cedergren, H., and D. Sankoff. 1974. Variable rules: Performance as a statistical reflection of competence. *Language* 50:333–55.

Cheshire, J. 1978. Present tense verbs in Reading English. In *Sociolinguistic patterns in British English*, ed. P. Trudgill, 53–67. London: Edward Arnold.

Davis, J. 1989. Distinguishing language contact phenomena in ASL interpretation. In *The sociolinguistics of the Deaf community*, ed. C. Lucas, 85-102. San Diego, Calif.: Academic Press.

Fasold, R. 1993. Microcomputer VARBRUL 2 System, MS-DOS version.

Hanson, V. 1981. When a word is not the sum of its letters: Fingerspelling and spelling. In *Status Report on Speech Research* 67–68:145–55.

Hoopes, R. 1998. A preliminary examination of pinky extension: Suggestions regarding its occurrence, constraints, and function. In *Pinky extension and eye gaze: Language use in Deaf communities,* ed. Ceil Lucas, 3–17. Sociolinguistics in Deaf Communities series, vol. 4. Washington, D.C.: Gallaudet University Press.

Klima, E., and U. Bellugi. 1979. *The signs of language.* Cambridge, Mass.: Harvard University Press.

Labov, W. 1972. *Sociolinguistic patterns.* Philadelphia, Penn.: University of Pennsylvania Press.

———. 1981. What can be learned about change in progress from synchronic description? In *Variation Omnibus*, ed. D. Sankoff and H. Cedergren, 184–92. Edmonton, Alberta: Linguistic Research.

Liddell, S., and R. Johnson. 1989. American Sign Language: The phonological base. *Sign Language Studies* 64:195–277.

Lucas, C. 1995. Sociolinguistic variation in ASL: The case of DEAF. In *Sociolinguistics in Deaf communities,* ed. C. Lucas, 3–25. Sociolinguistics in Deaf Communities series, vol. 1. Washington, D.C.: Gallaudet University Press.

Lucas, C., R. Bayley, M. Rose, and A. Wulf. 2002. Location variation in American Sign Language. *Sign Language Studies* 2(4): 407–440.

Lucas, C., R. Bayley, and C. Valli, eds. 2001. *Sociolinguistic Variation in ASL.* Sociolinguistics in Deaf Communities series, vol. 7. Washington, D.C.: Gallaudet University Press.

Lucas, C., and C. Valli. 1992. *Language Contact in the American Deaf Community.* San Diego: Academic Press.

Malloy, C., and J. Donner. 1995. Variations in ASL discourse: Gender differences in the use of cohesive devices. In *Communication Forum,* ed. L. Byers, J. Chaiken, and M. Mueller, vol. 4, 183–205. Washington, D.C.: Department of ASL, Linguistics, and Interpreting, Gallaudet University.

Mansfield, D. 1993. Gender differences in ASL: A sociolinguistic study of sign choices by Deaf native signers. In *Communication Forum,* ed. E. A. Winston, vol. 2, 86–95. Washington D.C.: Department of ASL, Linguistics and Interpreting, Gallaudet University.

McMurtrie, J. 1993. Conversational analysis of characteristics of gender differences in feedback in ASL. In *Communication Forum,* ed. E. A. Winston, vol. 2, 125–31. Washington, D.C.: Department of ASL, Linguistics and Interpreting, Gallaudet University.

Nowell, E. 1989. Conversational features and gender in ASL. In *The sociolinguistics of the Deaf community,* ed. C. Lucas, 273–88. San Diego: Academic Press.

Padden, C. 1991. The acquisition of fingerspelling by deaf children. In *Theoretical issues in sign language research,* ed. P. Siple and S. Fischer, 191–210. Chicago: University of Chicago Press.

Rand, D., and D. Sankoff. 1999. GoldVarb Version 2.1. Université de Montréal, Centre de Recherches Mathématiques.

Stokoe, W., D. Casterline, C. Croneberg. 1965. *A Dictionary of American Sign Language.* Silver Spring, Md.: Linstok Press.

Trudgill, P. 1972. Sex, covert prestige, and linguistic change in the urban British English of Norwich. *Language in Society* 1:179–95.

Valli, C., and C. Lucas. 1992. *Linguistics of American Sign Language.* Washington, D.C.: Gallaudet University Press.

Wilcox, S. 1992. *The phonetics of fingerspelling.* Philadelphia: John Benjamins.

Wulf, A. 1998. Gender related variation in ASL signing space. Guided research paper, Gallaudet University, Washington, D.C.

Zimmer, J. 1989. Toward a description of register variation in American Sign Language. In *The sociolinguistics of the Deaf community,* ed. C. Lucas, 253–72. San Diego: Academic Press.

Part 2 Language Contact and Bilingualism

So, Why Do I Call This English?

Bruce A. Sofinski

For the last thirty years, the terms *interpreting* and *transliterating* have been used to identify two disciplines common to assessment and education within the broader field of sign language interpreting (Solow 1981; Frishberg 1990). Historically, the various definitions of sign language interpreting have included working between the languages of (spoken) English and American Sign Language, or ASL (Solow 1981; Colonomos 1992; Frishberg 1990; Stewart, Schein, and Cartwright 1998; Solow 2001; RID 2001). Until relatively recently, the various published definitions of transliterating have agreed that the practitioner works between spoken English and some form of manually coded English, or MCE (Solow 1981; Frishberg 1990). Although more recent definitions of transliterating have expanded that definition to include various elements of English and ASL, most definitions continue to posit that transliteration is a "word-for-sign" representation of English using manual communication in "English order" (Stewart, Schein, and Cartwright 1998; Solow 2001; Kelly 2001).

Anecdotal accounts by many students, certified interpreters, and interpreter educators indicate that, although this latter definition of transliteration is representative of the literature in the field, it does not accurately describe what many competent transliterators do. In other words, while many consumers prefer and many situations lend themselves to a more word-for-sign or literal rendition of the spoken English source message, many other consumers and situations still call for a product that many peo-

This chapter was initiated as an independent study in the spring of 2000 as part of my graduate studies in linguistics at Gallaudet University. I thank Robert E. Johnson for his guidance and for his willingness to share his insight on ASL and his passion for the study of language. I also express my sincere appreciation to Ceil Lucas for all of the times she has gone to bat for me. Special thanks to Melanie Metzger, Scott Liddell, Nancy Yesbeck, and Laura Sanheim for our illuminating discussions with respect to various topics included in this chapter.

To my loving wife, Elaine, and my children—Jacob, Eliza, and Nicholas—I love you all very much. Thank you for giving me the opportunity to do something that I love.

ple would identify as more English-like, yet not a word-for-sign rendition. Although these products often follow the ordering of constituents that are common in English (e.g., subject-verb-object), they do not necessarily follow the order of elements contained in the spoken English source message. Additionally, except for instances where a literal conveyance is critical (e.g., proper names, titles), many competent transliterators (i.e., those who possess an RID Certificate of Transliteration) do not necessarily provide a literal rendition that provides a word-for-sign product mirroring the spoken source.

As the field of interpreting continues to mature, the literature is slowly moving away from a nearly absolute dependence on anecdotal accounts or personal theory to define interpreting and moving toward definitions that include more instances of scientific, empirically based descriptions and analyses. For interpreting, this trend has involved using various studies of ASL, including linguistic and sociolinguistic analyses, to describe the target for a sign language transliterator. The trend has also involved examining the product of the practitioner and the elements and strategies that he or she uses to work between English and ASL (Winston 1989; Siple 1993; Sofinski, Yesbeck, Gerhold, and Bach-Hansen 2001). Over the course of time, this in-depth examination of ASL has led to studies investigating instances of naturally occurring phenomena such as Pidgin Signed English, or PSE (Woodward 1973), also referred to as contact signing (Lucas and Valli 1992), including the identification of elements of English and ASL recurring in the data.

In contrast, the linguistic examination of an individual actually using one of these codes of manual communication designed to represent English has been lacking. Instead, the corpus of literature that presently exists largely comprises the published descriptions of the systems by the inventors of particular code: Seeing Essential English, or SEE 1 (Anthony 1971), Signing Exact English, or SEE 2 (Gustason, Pfetzing, and Zawolkow 1975), Linguistics of Visual English, or LOVE (Wampler 1971), and Signed English (Bornstein 1983).

In Padden's (1998) description of the ASL lexicon, she suggests that linguists have typically selected signs in their analysis of ASL grammatical structure that are considered to be native, relegating by default all other vocabulary to be considered part of "Sign English" (also expressed by others as "Signed English"). The result of this practice is the ill-defined linguistic description of "Sign English," which instead, has been debated more in terms of ideology than its component structural properties.

The present study is the linguistic examination of a sign language narrative, "How I met My Husband," that uses the elements described as contact signing (see appendix A for the full English translation). The selection of the narrative was based on several factors, including the narrative author's description of it as being "more English with a mix of ASL" (Personal communication, Beverly Bailey in a letter to Sofinski, September 2001) and the background of the signer (a deaf adult who attended a residential school for the deaf for thirteen consecutive years and married a deaf spouse, both of whom use this type of "sign language" as their primary mode of communication). The goal is to provide a detailed account of selected language elements used by a specific consumer who typically prefers sign language transliteration, as opposed to interpretation.

THE HISTORY OF INTERPRETING

Although the impetus of what was to become the Registry of Interpreters for the Deaf, Inc. (RID), the first organization to represent sign language interpreters in America, can be traced to a 1964 meeting at Ball State University, in Muncie, Indiana, people had been acting in the role of sign language interpreter in America for at least 150 years before then. These individuals had little if any training (no formal sign language interpreter training programs existed before RID); they were largely children of deaf adults (CODAs) or professionals, most notably, educators and counselors who worked in other fields providing services to individuals using sign language. Between the time of the Ball State conference and the first national sign language interpreter evaluation in 1972, the professional service delivery of sign language interpreting was recognized in law (Stewart, Schein, and Cartwright 1998).

The Difference between Interpreting and Transliterating

In 1972, the RID evaluation system formalized the notion of two disciplines within sign language interpreting—interpreting and transliterating. Interpreters work between ASL and spoken English whereas transliterators work between spoken English and English-based signing (RID 2001).

The Continuum

To better understand what is meant by English-based signing within the paradigm of manual communication, one must understand a prevailing theory of the last 30 years—the continuum. First posited in the 1970s, this concept of a continuum represented a range with ASL and English at polar ends. Throughout the 1980s, several publications outlined this concept, placing PSE, or contact signing, in the middle of the range. Baker-Shenk and Cokely called the concept the "bilingual continuum" (1980, 74) or the "ASL-English continuum" (77); Solow (1981, 2001) identifies this idea as the "Communication Continuum" (1981, 12; 2001, 16). In discussing language competencies necessary for interpreters, Frishberg (1990) stated that interpreters "must also have excellent sign language skills, including a range of variation from American Sign Language through a multitude of ways of incorporating English into a visual-gestural code" (26).

AMERICAN SIGN LANGUAGE (ASL)

In the description of this continuum theory, ASL is a naturally occurring language with a history, syntax, and grammatical structure separate and distinct from English. ASL is found primarily in the United States and Canada, and it "is a defining characteristic of the American Deaf community" (Moores 1994, 190). A critical mass of literature describes ASL, the community that uses this language, and the culture of this community (Stokoe, Casterline, and Croneberg 1965; Klima and Bellugi 1979; Liddell 1980; Padden and Humphries 1988; Smith, Lentz, and Mikos 1988; Rutherford 1993).

FORMS OF MANUALLY CODED ENGLISH (MCES)

At the other end of the continuum is English (i.e., the spoken variety that is commonly used in much of the United States and Canada). Placed in close proximity to English on the continuum are the MCEs. During the 1960s, an influx of federal funds promoting the development of methods intended to increase the effectiveness of teaching English to deaf children spurred the development of various MCE systems (Moores 1994). The four most widely documented efforts are Seeing Essential English (SEE 1), Signing Exact English (SEE 2), Linguistics of Visual English (LOVE), and Signed English (Bornstein 1973). Baker-Shenk and Cokely (1980) posit that these systems are codes, and as codes, linguists argue that they will never be able to adequately convey or completely represent the English language.

CONTACT SIGNING, OR PIDGIN SIGNED ENGLISH (PSE)

The area of the continuum between ASL and English is labeled with terms indicating a mixture of ASL and English elements. These terms include "contact variety" (Solow 2001) and "pidgin signed English" (Baker-Shenk and Cokely 1980).

PSE is a term coined in the early 1970s (Woodward 1973) and has been commonly used to refer to a natural phenomenon that occurs when two or more individuals who are bilingual and who possess varying levels of facility in both English and ASL communicate with one another. Lucas and Valli (1992) found that this phenomenon is more appropriately characterized in linguistic terms as language contact or contact signing because "contact signing is a third system resulting from the contact between ASL and English and consisting of features from both languages" (104). In addition to being naturally occurring, contact signing varies from artificially invented MCEs in two other important ways: (a) it is not intended to represent the structure of English, and (b) it is not linguistically prescriptive but, rather, is descriptive in that the incorporation of specific English and ASL features vary by individual use, depending on the situation and context (Baker-Shenk and Cokely 1980).

Lucas and Valli (1992) provide a list of English and ASL features occurring in contact signing that were identified in their data. These English elements include conjunctions (e.g., but, because); prepositions; verb with prepositions; invented morphemes (e.g., #ING, IT, I); mouthing of English words; English word order; and unusual initialization (e.g., R-elatives). Some ASL elements that were identified include nonmanual negation, gaze, pronouns, ASL word order, rhetorical question, lexical signs with no mouthing, locative verbs, and role shifting.

What was found in the corpus of Lucas and Valli's (1992) data was equally as critical to their work as what was not contained: "For example, even though some individuals use more ASL features than other individuals, we see very few examples of important ASL nonmanual syntactic markers such as occur with topicalization (with the accompanying word order)" (105). The accompanying word order that is alluded to is object-subject-verb, which requires accompanying nonmanual signals for the sentence to be grammatically acceptable in ASL (Liddell 1980).

Lucas and Valli (1992) used a judging system in which individuals with an extensive background in linguistics, called master judges, were asked to label twenty clips of discourse from the data as being "ASL" or "not ASL." Independently, a group of thirty people "who were Deaf ASL users who had learned ASL natively or at a very early age" (69) were asked to judge the same twenty clips in the same way. Five of these clips, judged as ASL by the master judges, were judged as "not ASL" by the majority of the Deaf ASL users. Four of these five clips share two important ASL features even though the overall structure was contact signing. "We suggest that establishment of topic and use of body shifting and eye gaze are salient ASL features that carry a lot of weight, even if the overall structure of a clip cannot be said to be ASL" (103).

Channels

A channel is any distinct mechanism for producing information important for accurate communication to occur. Various channels are used in communication (Davis 1989). For example, both the mouth (oral) and the ear (aural) channels are critical in communication using spoken English. In ASL, the mouth (oral) and hand (manual) channels are used to communicate.

ASL AND ENGLISH FEATURES FOUND IN THE MOUTH CHANNEL

In Davis's (1989) investigation of language contact phenomena in ASL interpretation, occurrences in the mouth channel was one area of focus in which he identified three different features. First, "full English mouthing" is the complete "pronunciation" of an English word, generally without voice. In contrast, the second feature, "reduced English mouthing," is the partial pronunciation of an English word, still without voice. Finally, "lexicalized mouthing" is the severely reduced mouthing of an English word that accompanies an ASL sign.

Similar to Davis's "lexical mouthing" is the concept of "word pictures" found in Sign Language of the Netherlands (SLN) (Schermer 1990). As described in Johnson (1994), "word pictures" are actually features of ASL that are influenced by English mouthing.

These facial gestures . . . are to be distinguished from attempts to gloss each sign with an exact English mouth movement . . . Some word pictures, such as the facial movement accompanying HAVE or that accompany LARGE, are linked strongly to specific lexical signs and occur almost invariantly, while other seems to be more variable in their occurrence. (13)

Adverbials are another mouth channel feature noted in the literature. These mouth movements are a basic element of ASL and provide information similar in function to English adverbs (Baker-Shenk and Cokely 1980).

ASL AND ENGLISH FEATURES FOUND IN THE HAND CHANNEL

Handshape, location, and movement were the three parameters of ASL signs identified by Stokoe, Casterline, and Croneberg (1965). In addition, palm orientation is a fourth manual parameter of ASL lexical items.

Padden (1998) provides examples of vocabulary in the ASL lexicon. In this description, native vocabulary notably includes classifier structures, plain and agreement verbs, adjectival predicates, and the pronominal system. However, Padden's description further illuminates the occurrence of foreign vocabulary in ASL. Padden posits that loan signs (Battison 1978), name signs, sign-fingerspell compounds, and sets of initialized signs (e.g., signs representing the seven days of the week, signs for colors) all share a common origin in the American fingerspelling system.

Although English features per se do not occur in the manual channel, gestural, or extralinguistic, features are important to communication by people who use spoken English. In addition, occurrences of "English influence," such as Padden's foreign vocabulary, are found in the hand channel.

In spoken English, gestures frequently co-occur with speech to provide more precise information (Scott Liddell, February 2000, personal communication). For example, pointing in the specific direction of an item that can be seen in the immediate surroundings while simultaneously saying "I want that one!" identifies the precise item that is the object of the speaker's desire.

English influence in the hand channel of a contact signing product can also be seen in other forms, including (a) syntactical influence in word order (especially when "full English mouthing" co-occurs in the mouth channel) and (b) influence during particular events in fingerspelling when there is an intentional representation of English orthography using ASL signs (Davis 1989).

Borrowing, Codeswitching, and Code-Mixing

Borrowing occurs between the phonological systems of two languages. In contrast, lexical initialization is an example of ASL morphemes being used to represent an English orthographic event (Davis 1989 in Lucas and Valli 1992).

Codeswitching is a term used when bilinguals literally change from one language to another during a conversation. During contact signing, codeswitching would necessitate one who is signing to stop signing and begin speaking. This phenomenon generally occurs intersententially. In contrast, code-mixing occurs when elements of both languages coming into contact are produced simultaneously. Code-mixing can also apply when the "shifting" between the languages occurs intrasententially (Lucas and Valli 1992).

Borrowing, codeswitching, and code-mixing are all terms that have been used to describe contact between ASL and English. These are important concepts to consider when discussing the existence of English in a manual form rather than English in a form that is spoken or represented orthographically.

METHODOLOGY

Selection of Narrative

The narrative selected for analysis is a signed narrative that is two minutes and twelve seconds long—one that was predominantly viewed as "more English-like" by competent, working sign language interpreters and interpreter educators who viewed the selection. This narrative is demonstrative of the type of English-like signing that is used by many consumers of sign language transliteration services.

About the Signer and Addressee

The signer, whom I shall call Mary, was born and raised in the suburbs of Philadelphia where she matriculated at the Pennsylvania School for the Deaf (PSD) in Mt. Airy. Mary entered PSD at the age of five and lived in the PSD dorms for the next thirteen years until her graduation. When asked where she grew up, Mary stated, "In dorm all my life . . . (from 1945–1957)."

The communication mode for Mary's experience is consistent with other accounts of the time. In class, the use of any type of manual communication or gesture was forbidden, and only speech was allowed. Outside of class, Mary used "ASL" everywhere else.

Mary was born deaf, the cause of the deafness being unknown. She characterized her own use of sign language while at PSD as "home sign and ASL . . . before [I] got older." Mary describes her use of sign language as an adult to be "ASL and English mix together." She illustrated the difference between English and ASL, explaining that English is "I will go to the store" whereas ASL is "Go to store."

Despite the fact that her hearing mother has lived with her for some time now, her parents never learned to sign. Her husband is deaf and uses a similar, English-like sign language as his primary mode of communication. Her three hearing children all sign to varying degrees, but Mary said they all sign "well enough to communicate on any subject." Mary is an active member of the Deaf community in her local area, a community in central Virginia where she has lived for more than forty years.

At the time of the taping, Mary was in her "late fifties." Her audience was a hearing man in his early thirties. Mary had known the addressee professionally and socially for approximately ten years. The addressee is fluent in ASL, being a nationally certified sign language interpreter (RID, Certificate of Interpretation [CI] and the Certificate of Transliteration [CT]) and having received an Advanced Plus rating on the Gallaudet University Sign Communication Proficiency Interview (SCPI) at about the time of the taping. Both Mary and the addressee consider each other to be friends. The story analyzed is typical of the type of signing Mary uses when regularly communicating with the addressee.

Procedure

The focus of the linguistic analysis of this product was narrowed to two channels: the hands (or manual channel) and the mouth (or oral channel). The features identified through an analysis of the manual and oral channels were charted and synchronously matched with each other; with the establishment of areas of space to be used as referents, which Liddell (1995) called tokens and surrogates; and with accompanying nonmanual signals (NMS) found in the following channels: head (tilt, turn, nod, and shake), eyebrow (raised, lowered), eye (actions of lid and pupil), and upper torso (including shoulders). The use of these two channels in this product was scripted using glossing and other conventions (Smith, Lentz, and Mikos 1988). Then, the instances and frequencies of occurrences within the oral and manual channels were noted and tabulated.

RESULTS

Examples of ASL and English Features in Contact Signing

Using the same characteristics as identified in segments of contact signing by Lucas and Valli (1992, 101–2), the analysis of this segment revealed that occurrences supporting a proportion of eight out of twelve of the English features and nine out of fourteen of the ASL features were identified. Examples of English features include the following: seven instances of conjunctions (but, and, because), including one without sign support (or); sixteen occurrences of prepositions (in, to, until, for, with); three instances of a verb with preposition ("go to school"); three instances of invented morphemes (I, #WAS); mouthing of English words (see section below); English word order, collocation ("go with another boy . . . date"); one instance of comparison ("like him better"); and three examples of unusual initialization (A-rea, V-ery, E-D-ucation).

Simultaneous Mixing of English and ASL Features

Perhaps the phenomenon in this analysis more striking than simply the occurrence of code-mixing is the preponderance of examples where an ASL feature and an English feature occur simultaneously in different channels of this product. This preponderance is striking in that most descriptions of contact signing portray a "switch" from ASL to English. In this case, the contact signing involves not a switch but, rather, features of both languages co-occurring, or mixing. This mixing can be seen in figures 1–9. Figure 1 provides a more detailed example with a description of the various English and ASL features that are found to be mixing, or co-occurring, in the segment.

In figure 1, one can see the following: (a) an example of a "dropped" subject (an ASL language feature); (b) an instance of a preposition (*to*, TO) co-occurring in both the mouth and manual channels; and (c) an instance of a past-tense verb (*went*), an English feature, co-occurring with the ASL

NMS-Head:
NMS-Eyebrow: $A \rightarrow$ gz-{SH} $A \rightarrow$
NMS-Torso:

Mouth:	went	to	school	Mount Airy
Manual:	GO TO##[SCHOOL]	TO	SCHOOL M-T	A-I-R-Y

English Translation: (grew up in Pennsylvania.) *I went to school in Mt. Airy.*
Note: Mt. Airy is an Eastern suburb of Philadelphia.

FIGURE 1. *An example of code-mixing*

verb GO-TO, which is locatively influenced by the token [SCHOOL], both ASL features (GO-TO##[SCHOOL]).

However, the simultaneous production of English and ASL elements is not limited to this example. In fact, this type of phenomenon occurs abundantly in these data. For a clearer description of the use of English words and ASL features in the product, several segments of the synchronous gloss transcription are included in figure 1.

Mouth Channel Features

FOUR MOUTH MOVEMENT FEATURES CO-OCCURRING WITH SIGN SUPPORT
The mouth channel was descriptively analyzed for its use of four distinct features: full English mouthing, reduced English mouthing, lexicalized mouthing, and adverbials. In every instance, these four features were coproduced with an occurrence in the manual channel.

Of the 174 lexical items that were manually produced, 150 (or 86.21 percent) were produced with full English mouthing simultaneously occurring through the mouth channel. These mouthed English items included the following (see table 1 as well as figures 2 and 3): (a) ten occurrences of past-tense verbs (went, grew, met, was, told); (b) two instances where two English words occurred synchronously with a single ASL sign (*grew up*, RAISE and *don't care*, DON'T-MIND); and (c) nine instances of English pronouns being mouthed over PRO.X or POSS.X signs (*his* mouthed over POSS.3-WREN, *I* mouthed over PRO.1, *him* mouthed over PRO.3, and *me* mouthed over PRO.1).

TABLE 1. *Mouth Channel Features Co-Occurring with Signs in Hand Channel*

Mouth Channel Feature	Occurrences Identified Out of 174 Items	Percentage
Full English mouthing	150	86.21
Reduced English mouthing	7	4.02
Lexical mouthing/word pictures	6	3.45
Adverbials	4	2.3
None discerned	7	4.02
Total	174	100.00

SIGN SPACE 2–3

(WREN) [SCHOOL]	NMS-Head					
	Eye/Brow:	*A* →				
	Torso:		{shift away from (WREN)}			
	Mouth:	senior		I	was	freshman
	Manual:	SENIOR		PRO.1	#WAS	F-R-E-S-H-M-A-N
▲						

English Translation: (My husband Wren was a) *senior; I was a freshman!*

FIGURE 2. *Example showing the mouthing of English words, an ASL pronoun, and the use of nonmanuals*

NMS-Head:					
NMS-Eye/Brow:	*A* →		**(ec/gz)*	*gz-(wren)*	**(ec/gz)*
NMS-Torso:					
Mouth:	[meet]	@ there		[sweetheart]	
Manual:	MEET##[SCHOOL]	@	*	GO-STEADY	

English Translation: *We met at school, and we "went steady."*

FIGURE 3. *Example showing reduced English mouthing, gaze, and "dropped" subject and object*

SIGN SPACE *1–4*

(WREN)	[SCHOOL]	NMS-Head:		(lean forward) pos
		NMS-Eye/Brow:	*	*(gz) A* →
		NMS-Torso:		
		Mouth:	* I met	Wren
		Manual:	* @ MEET	W-R-E-N
			*	WH: THERE-[SCHOOL]

▲

English Translation: (I grew up at school.) *I met Wren there.*

FIGURE 4. *Example of "dropped" subject in the manual channel*

USE OF FULL ENGLISH MOUTHING WITHOUT SIGN SUPPORT

A fifth feature, full English mouthing without sign support, also was noted in the product (see figure 4). Seven instances of full English mouthing without sign support were noted. These mouthed English items included the following: (a) two subjects (it, that); (b) four verbs, including one infinitive (to) and two copulas (was, 's); and (c) one conjunction (or).

Manual Channel

GRAMMATICAL CATEGORIES OF SIGNS

The manual channel was analyzed for instances of grammatical use: category, function, and order of grammatical constituents. Also, several instances of foreign vocabulary in ASL (Padden 1998) were also noted, including three instances of lexicalized pronouns (#HE, #HIM) and four occurrences of invented morphemes (Lucas and Valli 1992), which included two instances of lexicalized copulas (#WAS) and two instances of initialized pronouns (I).

In addition, several instances of ASL features were noted, including ASL word order (see figure 6) and eight occurrences where the subject of a sentence was "dropped," or not represented by a lexical item in the manual channel (as contained in figure 4).

EVIDENCE OF SALIENT ASL FEATURES

Lucas and Valli (1992) identified that four segments were contained within their study that were considered to be "ASL" by the master judges, even though the overall structure of each segment was contact signing, but

NMS-Head:	*tl*-forward *tl*-forward	*ht*-right, left, right	*tl*-forward
			ht-side to side

Eye/Brow:	*A* →		(*ec*)	*squint*	(pause)
Torso:					

			(hands clasped)		
Mouth:	I stay	until 57	(long pause)	How	
Manual:		I STAY-[PSD]	UNTIL 57.	*	How	*

English Translation: (My husband stayed at Pennsylvania School for the Deaf until h graduation in 1954.) *I stayed until 1957. So, how* (did we wind up getting married? H told me, "You . . .)

FIGURE 5. *An example showing an ASL rhetorical question, English preposition use, and invented morphemes*

NMS-Head:	*A* →			*			
Eye/Brow:	*A* →						
Torso:	*A* →						
Mouth:	already know	how	sign	they	require (none) (none)	strict
Manual:	FINISH KNOW	HOW	SIGN*	THERE??	[CLARKE] REQUIRE ONLY ORAL	#STRIC

English Translation: (He) *already knew sign language. The Clarke school had a stri⟨ requirement of oral communication only.* (No sign language was allowed.)

FIGURE 6. *An example showing ASL word order*

SIGN SPACE 3–3

(WREN) [SCHOOL]	NMS-Head:	nod++	nod	
	Eye/Brow: *A* →	eg-[RICH]	*A* →	t –
	NMS-Torso:	*ln*-forward		
[RICH]	Mouth: Wren	born	here	Richmond.
	Manual: W-R-E-N	BORN##[RICH]	HERE##[RICH]	RICHMOND

▲

English Translation: *Wren was born here in Richmond.*

FIGURE 7. *Example showing use of referents and gaze*

that were considered to be "not ASL" by the Deaf ASL users. Lucas and Valli posited that salient ASL features incorporated into these segments caused this conflict between judging groups. These features are the establishment of topic and the use of body shifting and eye gaze (see figure 7).

Liddell (1995) conceptualizes the establishment of areas of space as referents in two different ways. A "token" is more typical of what has been described as a referent—an area of space with no specific physical features. In Mary's narrative, setting up "the school," later identified as "PSD," is an example of a token. In contrast, a "surrogate" is an area of space that is perceived to have specific physical features—as if a person were really occupying that area of space.

The identification of distinct physical clusters of signs produced in different locations was identified through a literal mapping of the signing space on the television screen. In "How I Met My Husband," seven of these clusters were identified (see figure 8).

These clusters of sign production, noted in figure 8, occurred at the locations where the signs were physically produced. The groupings were labeled to identify neutral space as well as a total of six clusters relating to three tokens and one surrogate identified in the discourse. Each of these clusters represents at least one group of signs that are either (a) pointing at or directed toward a representation of the same semantic entity—designated by -[TOKEN] or -(SURROGATE)—or (b) locatively influenced by the same semantic entity—designated by ##[TOKEN] or ##(SURROGATE). In other words, signs relating to Mary's husband (Wren) were produced in

-[CLARKE]
      ##[CLARKE] and [PSD]
                                     -(WREN)

-[PSD] and sometimes   ##(WREN)
-[CLARKE]

           neutral

-[RICHMOND]

Note: The symbols ## and - as well as the word ***neutral*** indicate the approximate physical locations of these clusters as noted on the video monitor.

FIGURE 8. *Physical placement of signs in clusters*

one of two locations. Both of these locations were in relative proximity to each other when compared to the placements of all seven clusters.

Areas of sign production that were locatively influenced by the existence of a token or surrogate (indicated by ##) were produced between the "neutral area" and the token or surrogate by which they were influenced. Areas of sign production that were either pointing at or directed toward a token or surrogate (indicated by -) were produced in another area further from "neutral" and closer to the token or surrogate.

THE ESTABLISHMENT AND IDENTIFICATION OF REFERENTS

Lucas and Valli (1992) further describe the identification of referents prior to their use. They state that "a topic must be established at a point in space *before* it can be talked about using whatever structure" (95, emphasis added). In contrast, although Mary obviously establishes referents in space and consistently incorporates them into her narrative, she does not always establish the topic at a point in space prior to a sign being influenced by its existence.

For example, in figure 9, the sign GO-TO is directed toward the area subsequently identified in the discourse as SCHOOL and later specified as PSD.

DISCUSSION

As one of a large number of people who have learned ASL or "sign language" during the last twenty years, this researcher has been overwhelmed by the preponderance of published information and seemingly endless

SIGN SPACE *1-2*

[SCHOOL]	NMS-Head:			
	NMS-Eye/Brow:	$A \rightarrow$		
	NMS-Torso:			
	Mouth:	went	to	school
	Manual:	GO-TO##[SCHOOL]	TO	SCHOOL

▲

English Translation: (I) *went to school* (in Mt. Airy).

FIGURE 9. *Evidence of token influencing direction of verb prior to overt identification of referent*

debate that relates to certain ideologies or persuasions rather than to linguistic or communicative descriptions of ASL or "Sign English." For example, in the present study of the narrative "How I Met My Husband," there are undoubtedly elements of English influence that proponents of one ideology or another can point to and say, "See, this is English!" However, the evidence found in this study simply does not support this claim.

Mouth Movements in Isolation

Although one can find obvious English influence in the mouth channel during this narrative, as attested to by the proliferation of "full English mouthing" and "reduced English mouthing" in the mouth channel of the product, a synchronous view of elements found only in the mouth channel does not result in the use of grammatically correct English. Figure 10 shows a script of mouth movements contained in the segment.

I grow up in Pennsylvania. Went to school Mount Airy in Philadelphia, in E . . . area East around. Grew up there. I met Wren. Wren go to school, too. That's how we met when Wren was a see . . . senior, senior. I was freshman.

Meet there. Sweetheart. Then he grad. Me still stay school 'til 1957.

It was funny. Wren born here Richmond, but moth-fath send him go to PSD school. That's how I met there.

One year later, his moth-fath *(ADVERBIAL)* want *(ADVERBIAL)* put Clark-ee Mass for oralism, and went to Clark-ee Mass school to talk with principal or "super" find that Wren can't enter school because he already know how sign. They require strict.

His moth-fath very upset. Wren don't care. Say happy where in our school, because have voke, have play sport. Where in Clarke *(ADVERBIAL)* voke, no sport, just school . . . ed-you . . . not right.

So, Wren prefer to stay until finish. I stay until '57. How? He told, "You go with other boy, date, because just young." *(ADVERBIAL)* but I like him better . . . for me.
(ADVERBIAL) . . . mare . . . move.

FIGURE 10. *Script of mouth movements from "How I Met My Husband"*

Punctuation, upper and lower case, and use of paragraphs are used to reflect the presence of nonmanual features indicating syntactic groupings (phrases and clauses) within the product.

English Influence on ASL Use Prior to the Development of MCEs

Contemporary terms such as *ASL, contact signing,* and *MCE* are relatively recent coinages. Padden and Humphries (1988) report that Deaf people in earlier decades recognized differences in signing but did not use these terms. Padden (1998) mentions the existence of a medium (film and videotape) for evidence of English influence on the use of sign language by fluent signers even before the advent of MCEs in the 1960s and 1970s. For example, the movies *A Cake of Soap* (1961) and *The Neighbor* (1963), films made by Ernest Marshall in the early 1960s, include numerous instances of English influence such as the concept of initialization (V-ery, L-ife, F-ind); English mouthing (*hotel-house* for FLAG^HOUSE); and the incorporation of English syntactic and morphological structure into a signed product (FIGHT OVER TREE). Padden characterizes the instances of initialized signs such as those indicated in the movies above as foreign vocabulary in ASL. Regardless of how they are characterized, however, all of these instances are also examples of English influence in the form of code-mixing.

Areas for Further Research

A detailed linguistic description of different varieties of naturally occurring contact signing. Particularly interesting is the delineation provided by Padden and Humphries (1988) differentiating "Sign English" and "various manual English systems." However, Mary's product lacks many of the features commonly described as being found in a form of MCE. Is this lack of features a common characteristic to most varieties of contact signing?

Effect on the definition and instruction of sign language transliteration. What implications does a product like Mary's have with respect to sign language transliteration? If the assertions of Baker-Shenk and Cokely (1980) and Padden and Humphries (1988) are correct (i.e., that the major difference between Sign English and

MCEs is that the former is naturally occurring and the latter is invented), then do these differences represent different varieties under the umbrella of ASL or English or interpretation? Outside of the training and testing environments, does the separate discipline of transliteration actually exist?

Patterns of English mouthing without sign support. In this study, seven instances of English mouthing without sign support were noted. Does a general pattern within contact signing (i.e., nouns, verbs, subjects) occur for this phenomenon?

Perception of a product being more English-like or ASL-like. Lucas and Valli (1992) investigated deaf people's perceptions of a product of another signer (i.e., was the product "ASL" or "not ASL?"). The standing of the signer in the Deaf community (i.e., deaf, hearing, Deaf from a Deaf family, etc.) appeared to have an effect on the viewer's perception. What if the hearing status of the signer is unknown? Do deaf people and hearing people who are fluent in sign language then have different perceptions of the same product?

CONCLUSION

So, why did I call this narrative product English? The above examples clearly show that Mary's narrative product contains a mixture of English and ASL features. This product contains uses of prepositions and the copula, features of English not shared by ASL. Likewise, instances of classifier predicates were identified, an ASL feature that is not shared by English. Additionally, four different types of mouth movements were identified in this product: two are English features, and two are ASL features. This description is consistent with the one of contact signing offered by Lucas and Valli (1992).

These data strongly suggest that the type of features (English or ASL) in the mouth and manual channels may guide the viewer's perception of which language has the most influence over the product as opposed to the signer actually "shifting" between the languages of ASL and English. This possibility is consistent with Lucas and Valli's claim that the existence of salient ASL features (use of space for referents and body shifting with gaze) causes a conflict when one tries to judge whether a segment is "ASL" or "not ASL."

Additionally, English is a naturally occurring spoken language with an accompanying standardized orthographic system that cannot be traced with any degree of certainty to any one individual or group of developers. However, all of these MCEs have been artificially created during the last forty years for specific use in the educational setting as a tool to teach English to deaf children. The fact that one can find evidence of English influence on ASL prior to the creation of MCEs indicates that Mary's product is potentially an example of a third system (Lucas and Valli 1992) and may even be ASL-based rather than English-based.

The data also clearly show that Mary is bilingual. For example, she demonstrates the difference between the same verb in different tenses. Initially, she mouths the verb "grow up" and accompanies her mouthing with the ASL signs GROW and #UP. Several lines later, she uses a different ASL sign (RAISE) to convey the same concept but, this time, co-produces mouthing for "grew up"—the same English verb as before, but in the past tense.

Contrary to popular anecdotal description, in Mary's product, English and ASL features are simultaneously co-produced in different channels. In reality, this contact signing product is not English but, rather, appears to be marked by various English influences in the mouth and manual channels. This researcher posits that many people base their perception of a product as being more "English-like" or more "ASL-like" on the features contained within the oral and manual channels because these channels are where they can most readily find the "most clear evidence" of an English influence, often paying little attention to the existence of simultaneously co-occurring ASL features.

REFERENCES

Anthony, D. 1971. *Seeing Essential English*. Greeley: University of Northern Colorado.

Baker-Shenk, C., and D. Cokely. 1980. *American sign language: A teacher's resource text on grammar and culture*. Silver Spring, Md.: T.J. Publishers.

Battison, R. 1978. *Lexical borrowing in American Sign Language*. Silver Spring, Md.: Linstok Press.

Bornstein, H. 1973. A description of some current sign systems designed to represent English. *American Annals of the Deaf* 118:454–63.

Bornstein, H., K. Saulnier, and L. Hamilton, eds. 1983. *The comprehensive signed English dictionary*. Washington, D.C.: Gallaudet University Press.

A Cake of Soap. 1963. Directed by E. Romero, Independent Theatrical and Cinema Club for the Deaf. Ernest Marshall Films. Gallaudet University Archives, Washington, D.C. Videocassette.

Colonomos, B. 1992. Process in interpreting and transliteration. Teleconference, 27 March, coordinated by Front Range Community College, Westminster, Colorado.

Davis, J. 1989. Distinguishing language contact phenomena in ASL interpretation. In *The sociolinguistics of the Deaf community,* ed. C. Lucas, 85–102. New York: Academic Press.

Frishberg, N. 1990. *Interpreting: An introduction.* Silver Spring, Md.: Registry of Interpreters for the Deaf.

Gustason, G., D. Pfetzing, and E. Zawolkow. 1975. Signing Exact English. Alameda, Calif.: Modern Signs Press.

Johnson, R. 1994. Possible influences on bilingualism in early ASL acquisition. *Teaching English to Deaf Students* 10(2):9–17.

Kelly, J. 2001. *Transliterating: Show me the English!* Alexandria, Va.: RID Press.

Klima, E., and U. Bellugi. 1979. *The signs of language.* Cambridge, Mass.: Harvard University Press.

Liddell, S. 1980. *American Sign Language syntax.* The Hague: Mouton.

———. 1995. Real, surrogate, and token space: Grammatical consequences in ASL. In *Language, gesture, and space,* ed. K. Emmorey and J. Reilly, 19–41. Hillsdale, N.J.: Lawrence Erlbaum Associates.

Lucas, C., and C. Valli. 1992. *Language contact in the American Deaf community.* San Diego, Calif.: Academic Press.

Moores, D. 1994. *Educating the Deaf: Psychology, principles, and practices.* 4th ed. Boston: Houghton Mifflin.

The Neighbor. 1961. Directed by E. Marshall, Independent Theatrical and Cinema Club for the Deaf. Ernest Marshall Films. Gallaudet University Archives, Washington, D.C. Videocassette.

Padden, C. 1998. The ASL lexicon. *Sign Language and Linguistics* 1:1, 39–64.

Padden, C., and T. Humphries. 1988. *Deaf in America: Voices from a culture.* Cambridge, Mass.: Harvard University Press.

Registry of Interpreters for the Deaf (RID). 2001. "Description of Rating Criteria for the CI and CT Performance Tests." RID web site, http://www.rid.org/crit.html

Rutherford, S. 1993. *A study of American Deaf folklore.* Burtonsville, Md.: Linstok Press.

Schermer, T. 1990. *In search of language: Influences from spoken Dutch on Sign Language of the Netherlands.* Delft, Netherlands: Eburon.

Siple, L. 1993. Interpreters' use of pausing in voice to sign transliteration. *Sign Language Studies* 79:147–80.

Smith, C., E. Lentz, and K. Mikos. 1988. *Signing naturally: Student workbook, level 1*. San Diego, Calif.: DawnSignPress.

Sofinski, B. A., N. A. Yesbeck, S. C. Gerhold, and M. C. Bach-Hansen. 2001. Features of voice-to-sign transliteration by educational interpreters. *Journal of Interpretation* 47–59.

Solow, S. 1981. *Sign language interpreting: A basic resource book*. Silver Spring, Md.: National Association of the Deaf.

———. 2001. *Sign language interpreting: A basic resource book*. Rev. ed. Silver Spring, Md.: National Association of the Deaf.

Stewart, D., J. Schein, and B. Cartwright. 1998. *Sign language interpreting: Exploring its art and science*. Boston: Allyn and Bacon.

Stokoe, W., D. Casterline, and C. Croneberg. 1965. *A dictionary of American Sign Language on linguistic principles*. Washington, D.C.: Gallaudet University Press.

Wampler, D. 1971. *Linguistics of visual English*. Pamphlet.

Winston, E. 1989. Transliteration: What's the message? In *The sociolinguistics of the Deaf community*, ed. C. Lucas, 147–64. New York: Academic Press.

Woodward, J. 1973. Some characteristics of Pidgin Sign English. *Sign Language Studies* 3:39–46.

How I Met My Husband

I grew up in Pennsylvania. I went to school in Mt. Airy, which is an eastern suburb of Philadelphia. I grew up there, and that's where I met Wren. He went to the same school. That's how we met when Wren was a senior and I was a freshman! We met and then we went steady for a while. Then, he graduated and I stayed at the school until my graduation in 1957.

It's really funny that we met there, because Wren was born here, in Richmond, Virginia, but his parents sent him to the Pennsylvania School for the Deaf (PSD). So, that's why we got the chance to meet at school.

After one year at PSD, Wren's parents looked into transferring him to the Clarke oral school in Massachusetts. They went on site to the Clarke school grounds and met with either the principal or superintendent of the school only to find out that he could not attend Clarke because he already knew how to sign. At the Clarke school there was strict enforcement of the oral-only approach. His parents were very upset at these developments, but it didn't bother Wren. He said he was happy at our school because we had vocational opportunities and sports teams in which he could participate, whereas the Clarke school didn't have these extracurricular opportunities. They focused solely on academics, and that's just not right!

So, he preferred to stay at the Pennsylvania School for the Deaf until his graduation in 1954. I graduated in 1957.

So how did we end up together? He told me, "you date and go with other boys because you're still young," but I liked him better. I knew that he was the one for me! Eventually we got married and moved to Richmond.

Transcription Conventions

▲ = sight line direction of signer

A = eye gaze to addressee [*reduced English mouthing*]

"X" = handshape represents first English letter of GLOSS

* = NMS to indicate a break at end of constituent

( ) = TOKEN

[ ] = SURROGATE

-[ ] = sign pointed at or directed towards (TOKEN) or [SURROGATE]

#WAS = lexicalized fingerspelling

= body oriented so production of sign influenced by location of (TOKEN) or [SURROGATE]

gz = eye gaze

{SH} = strong hand

{WH} = weak hand

@ = feature synchronously occurs here

ht = head turn

n = neutral

ec = eyes close

tl = head tilt

ln = lean

?? = [PSD] "as" [CLARKE]

SIGN SPACE = the physical space in which signs are produced

+ = sign repeated once

++ = sign repeated twice

pos = NMS indicating affirmation

(In English translation sections): ( ) = product coming before or after the actual transcription; italic text = translation for actual transcription.

Part 3 **Discourse Analysis**

Grounded Blend Maintenance as a Discourse Strategy

Paul Dudis

This chapter examines ASL discourse involving classifier predicates and constructed action. A remarkable aspect of this discourse is that information previously provided by the hands and other parts of the body continues to be present despite changes in form. Specifically, a classifier predicate may, without detrimental effect to its meaning, be reduced in form by the production of another classifier predicate. In addition, a distinct sign may be produced while only a part of the classifier predicate is maintained. In these cases, the sign is produced quite differently from its citation form. This activity is particularly striking if the sign is one that does not ordinarily use space.

Fauconnier and Turner's (1996, 1998) framework of conceptual blending is used here to analyze the above discourse possibilities. Conceptual blending is a cognitive process involving elements from two separate input mental spaces, some of which are mapped onto a third space, resulting in a blend. The types of blends described in this paper are grounded blends, which are blends that involve elements within the signers' environment, including their own bodies (Liddell 1998, 2000). When signers are part of a grounded blend, which is commonplace in nearly every type of signed language discourse, addressees understand the signer or the signer's hands to be physically manifesting a particular concept; this manifestation exists only when the blend is active. Signers then have a number of choices with respect to the next step in discourse construction, each of which contributes a distinct narrative effect. One choice is maintenance of the blend by keeping particular mappings intact, which allows the blend to be developed further. This

This chapter is a revision of the paper "Maintenance and Development of Blended Space in ASL Narratives" presented at the 1998 Theoretical Issues in Sign Language Research conference at Gallaudet University. I am indebted to Scott Liddell for his guidance on my master's research project and ongoing related endeavors. I also wish to thank the anonymous reviewer whose comments and feedback led to a clearer description of ideas presented in this paper and Audrey Cooper for her editorial assistance.

discourse strategy enables changes to classifier predicate forms to occur while the element associated with the classifier predicate continues to be present in a meaningful way as discourse proceeds.

CONCEPTUAL BLENDING

Conceptual blending underlies many distinct phenomena in language and thought. Examples analyzed in other publications (Fauconnier and Turner 1996, 1998) include metaphor, riddle solving, and an otherwise impossible scenario involving individuals from different time periods who engage in a debate even though they do not speak the same language. Conceptual blending has also been shown to be a necessary device for comprehending certain jokes (Coulson 1996) and activities such as the game "trashcan basketball," which involves a crumpled piece of paper and a wastebasket (Coulson 2001). Instances of conceptual blending are pervasive in signed language discourse that involves indicating verbs and constructed action (Liddell 1995, 1998, 2000; Liddell and Metzger 1998).

Conceptual blending is a cognitive process that involves two separate mental-space inputs. These inputs comprise particular structures and elements, some of which are mapped onto a third mental space, creating the blend (Fauconnier and Turner 1996, 1998). Before describing this process, I will describe two types of mental spaces that serve as inputs for the blends analyzed in this paper. Mental spaces can be described as "constructs distinct from linguistic structures but built up in any discourse according to guidelines provided by the linguistic expressions" (Fauconnier 1994, 16). For example, during an astronomy talk about rockets in orbit presented in a spoken English environment, audience members might have access to one mental space that is labeled "base space" because the lecture is perceived as proceeding from this mental space. The act of lecturing establishes this base space; within the given lecture topic, the frame of "orbiting" structures this mental space, indicated in caps inside the box in figure 1. Conceptual entities within this mental space are introduced or identified by noun phrases but are not themselves linguistic items (Fauconnier 1994). In this case, the noun phrase *the rocket* identifies element **r** *rocket* in the base space.[1] Other elements may be inferred by the frame structure, as with

---

1. The bold letters label the element, and the italicized word (the element) is provided simply to aid memory.

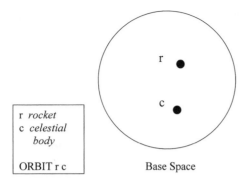

| r rocket |
| c celestial |
| body |
| ORBIT r c |

Base Space

Figure 1.

element **c** *celestial body*. Orbiting necessarily involves two entities, with one moving around the other. Element **r** fills the role of the object that is orbiting, and element **c** fills the role of the entity around which an object orbits. Even though no linguistic mention of planets or moons is made, members of the audience understand that, when rockets orbit, they do so around celestial bodies, so element **c** exists in the base space.

Not all mental spaces are associated with linguistic expressions. Real Space is another type of mental space where one has perceptual access to individuals, objects, and other entities within the physical environment (Liddell 1995). In the astronomy lecture example, the audience members' Real Space would consist of the professor and other elements in the immediate environment as perceived by the audience. If a member of the audience wishes to point to the professor or approach the professor to shake her hand, these actions would be guided by Real Space. The professor would not be available in Real Space (at least, not visually) if the lights were turned off and the room was totally dark or if she were to leave the room. If the audience has an image of the professor, it will not be grounded because the professor is not in their Real Space. The difference is groundedness. The base space described above is a nongrounded mental space. The base space elements **r** *rocket* and **c** *celestial body* do not have actual presence in the physical environment, so one cannot produce even pointing gestures toward them. Real Space is a grounded mental space, which allows one to direct pointing gestures toward all present elements (Liddell 1995).

Blended mental spaces can be either grounded or nongrounded, depending on whether Real Space is one of its input spaces (Liddell 1998, 2000). Elements of a nongrounded mental space that are mapped onto a physical element of Real Space generate a visible conceptual element that is unique to the blend. As an illustration, suppose that the professor from the previous example performs the following demonstration of a rocket's orbiting actions using a pencil. The professor holds the eraser end of the pencil, points the lead end upward, and moves the pencil in an upward-moving arc. Although the professor provides no explanation of this behavior, the audience understands that the pencil is being used to represent the immediate topic, a rocket. As the professor explains how rockets reach a certain orbit, she moves the pencil accordingly, and the audience also understands that "pencil as a rocket" is moving in an upward arc. When one sees the pencil in Real Space, independent of any conceptual blend, one will see only the pencil and not the "pencil as rocket." For example, a passerby walking past the lecture hall and seeing the professor move the pencil will not automatically understand that the pencil represents a rocket. In figure 2, the pencil in the Real Space portion of the mental-space diagram will always be a pencil to both the audience and the passerby. However, only those viewing the lecture will also see "the pencil as rocket" in addition to the pencil; this particular entity exists only in the blend, as shown in figure 2. This entity is labeled |rocket|, which follows the convention of labeling grounded mental-space elements with brackets. The |rocket| is not the base-space element **r**, and it is not a pencil. It exists by the mapping of element **r** onto the pencil. In this way, the professor is conferring a special conceptual status to the pencil that, by virtue of the mapping, now has a double value. When this blend is deactivated, the |rocket| will no longer continue to exist, and the pencil will have only a single value.

The |rocket| is not the only blended-space element in the rocket blend. Another grounded conceptual entity, |celestial body|, also exists in the blend. The existence of this entity is a result of the mapping of the base space element **c** onto the space in front of the professor. Unlike the |rocket|, the |celestial body| is not visible because, in this instance, the mapping does not involve a visible element in Real Space. Nevertheless, it is possible to make the |celestial body| visible. The professor could elect to use her fist as part of the rocket blend, map element **c** onto it, and thereby bring a visible |celestial body| into existence. Only then would a part of the professor's body be part of the blend.

Despite the differences in visibility, both |rocket| and |celestial body| have equal conceptual status. Although one probably could not appropriately say that the |rocket| has more conceptual presence than the |celestial body|, the |rocket| does have richer detail by virtue of the physical properties of the pencil. The pencil's cylindrical shape corresponds to that of the rocket, and its pointed lead corresponds to the nose of the rocket. The |celestial

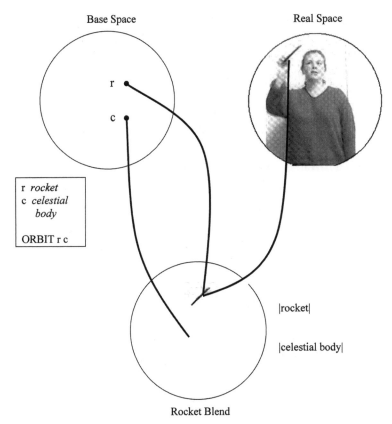

Base Space   Real Space

r

c

r *rocket*
c *celestial*
  body

ORBIT r c

|rocket|

|celestial body|

Rocket Blend

Figure 2.

body| is less rich in detail, but certain properties of element c—its spherical shape, for instance—are inherited by this invisible blended element. Furthermore, the audience will expect that the demonstrated interaction between the |rocket| and the |celestial body| conforms to their knowledge of rockets, celestial bodies, and the action of orbiting.

Finally, let us consider what an instance of a grounded blend in ASL discourse might look like. Suppose the same astronomy professor is conducting her lecture in ASL. Her discussion of orbiting rockets will produce the same base space as in the English lecture. To demonstrate the actions of the rocket, she produces an R classifier handshape with its fingertips pointing upward. She then moves it in an upward-moving arc. This activity results in a grounded blend similar to the rocket blend diagrammed in figure 2. The only difference between the two is the Real Space element involved in the mapping; in the ASL lecture, the base-space element r *rocket* is mapped on the R classifier handshape, producing the visible element |rocket|.

The ASL examples analyzed in this paper involve not only the signer's hands but also other parts of the signer's body. As will be demonstrated, this use of hands and other body parts allows for interesting discourse possibilities involving various types of grounded blends and other strategies available to the signer. Generally, the narrative goals of the signer and the physiological limits of the articulators affect the construction and flow of the signed language narrative. However, by using certain narration strategies, the signer is able to develop his or her narrative without sacrificing the desired narrative flow. One of these strategies involves continuous activation of a grounded blend by keeping particular mappings intact. This blend maintenance strategy is demonstrated in the following examples.

The Hunter Blend

The following examples are part of an ASL narrative about a hunter's encounter with a deer. In this narrative, the signer describes how the hunter is aiming his rifle when, to his delight, a deer emerges in front of him. The hunter follows the movement of this deer and prepares to shoot. This deer hunt narrative begins with transcription 1.

TRANSCRIPTION 1.

ONE FRIEND HUNT DEER.

"There was this friend who was hunting deer."

The act of narrating establishes a mental space, and the noun phrases ONE FRIEND and DEER set up two elements, **h** *hunter* and **d** *deer*, within this mental space (see figure 3). The plain verb HUNT brings the hunting frame into the mental space. The hunting frame necessarily consists of two roles,

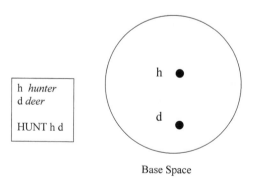

Base Space

Figure 3.

"hunter" and "prey." Element **h** fills the role of hunter, and element **d** fills the role of prey. Because the narrative proceeds from this mental space, it is labeled the base space. This base space is nongrounded. In addition to the base space, the signer's audience also has access to Real Space, where the audience sees the signer producing what is shown in transcription 1.

Soon after transcription 1 is signed, the signer demonstrates the hunter's action of aiming a rifle. This kind of demonstration has been termed "constructed action" by Winston (1991, 1992) and Metzger (1995). A classifier predicate, illustrated in figure 4, is produced as follows. The signer's hands are raised to near the shoulder level, each having a particular configuration. The left hand is configured with a C classifier handshape and positioned away from the signer. The right hand is configured with an X classifier handshape and is positioned near the chin. The signer is no longer facing the audience; instead, the signer's head is tilted down and to the right so the face is directed leftward, with eyes gazing in the same direction.

Here, the signer has created a grounded blend that is basically similar to the rocket blend. The signer provides no prior explanation of his or her behavior, yet this behavior cues the audience to construct a blend as follows. As figure 5 shows, the base-space element **h** *hunter* is mapped onto the signer, resulting in a visible blended element, the |hunter|. The audience understands the head tilt, eye gaze, and hand configurations to be the |hunter|'s. The blended element |hunter| exists only in the blend. It is distinct from the signer in Real Space and from element **h** *hunter* in the base space.

Without being given any explicit mention of a weapon, the audience also understands that some weapon exists in this blend. Their ability to determine the existence and the type of weapon is based on information given by the signer and the hunting frame. In addition to the roles of hunter

Figure 4.

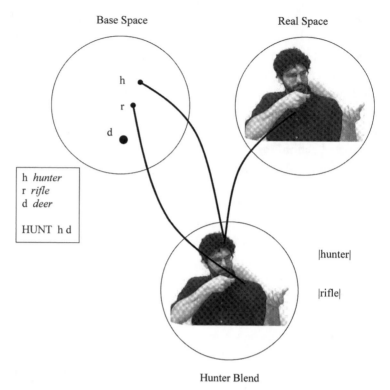

Base Space   Real Space

h   hunter
r   rifle
d   deer

HUNT h d

|hunter|

|rifle|

Hunter Blend

Figure 5.

and prey, the hunting frame also contains the means by which the hunter captures, maims, or kills the prey. The audience therefore expects that some kind of a hunting weapon is part of the narrative.

The details of the classifier predicate indicated by the signer's hand and other parts of the signer's body add further specification to the weapon. The weapon must be a two-handed weapon, with one hand at the trigger and the other supporting the longer barrel portion. Given that rifles, and not crossbows, are part of the prototypical hunting scene (at least from where this signer and audience hail), the audience is satisfied that they have all the details needed to conceptualize the hunting weapon. Indeed, no more details are available within either input space to further specify the weapon.

The hunting frame, which structures the base space and the physical information made by the signer, identifies the base-space element **r** *rifle* and its properties. This element **r** is mapped onto the empty space within the confines of the signer's hands, resulting in the blended element |rifle|. Unlike the |hunter|, the |rifle| is not visible because element **r** is not mapped onto a physical object in Real Space. Nevertheless, both blended elements are equally present.

Some Grounded Blend Discourse Strategies

After establishing the grounded blends, the signer continues the discourse by choosing one of several options with respect to the blends. As one option, the signer could return to the original posture that had been assumed before establishing the blend and could continue signing. This option would indicate to the audience that the mappings that activate the grounded blend are no longer intact, so no blended elements exist. These elements will exist only when the grounded blend they are part of is reactivated. For example, if the hunter blend were deactivated, then the next time the signer reassumes the posture of the |hunter|, the hunter blend would be reactivated.

Blend deactivation also can occur when the signer produces a different grounded blend. For instance, should the signer wish to develop the deer hunt narrative by indicating the appearance of a deer, he or she needs to produce signs or perform a number of changes that may deactivate the hunter blend. One possible result is shown in the Real Space portion of figure 6. The signer's posture changes to one where the back is straightened and the chest is thrust slightly outward. The X and C classifier handshapes each are replaced by a bent-V classifier handshape. These handshapes are positioned near the chest, palms facing downwards, right hand behind the left. The signer's head is now positioned so the face is directed to the right with a relaxed facial expression.

These changes cue the audience to deactivate the hunter blend and establish new grounded blends. In one of the blends, the base-space element d *deer* is mapped on the signer, resulting in a blended element |deer|. In this blend, the head position, eye gaze, facial expression, and posture all are understood to belong to the |deer|. In a separate blend, partial information from element d is mapped onto the classifier handshapes, resulting in the blended elements |front legs of the deer| and |rear legs of the deer|. Two separate but simultaneously active blends are necessary to understand the signer's demonstration, as shown in figure 6. A single blend, instead of this simultaneous use, forces the interpretation that the |deer|'s two front legs are raised, displaying two unnatural protrusions on the front hooves. This interpretation is obviously not intended by the signer. Therefore, when he or she demonstrates the actions of the deer, the

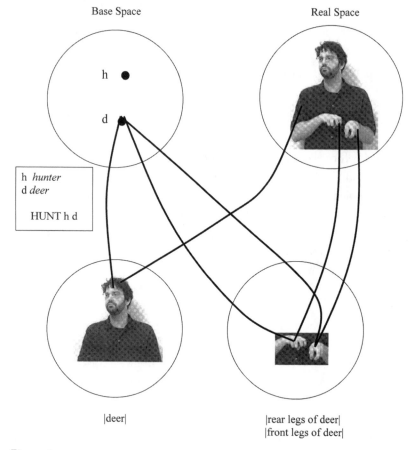

Base Space

Real Space

h hunter
d deer

HUNT h d

|deer|

|rear legs of deer|
|front legs of deer|

Figure 6.

signer's body is partitioned into different blends. This kind of blend contrasts with the hunter blend, where the signer's body and hands together contribute to the blend construction.

The establishment of two or more grounded blends allows for a common discourse practice. As demonstrated in Liddell and Metzger (1998), the signer may develop his or her narrative by alternating between blends, which involves successive and possibly extended deactivation and reactivation of blends. This kind of sequence has a cinematic effect of jumping among camera shots. In the deer narrative described above, the first camera shot is on the narrator in Real Space, the second on the |hunter|, and the third on the |deer|. Continued narration can involve further jumping among any of these shots or even the adding of new ones.

This discourse strategy of performing successive deactivations and reactivations has a place in signed narratives. At times, however, the signer may choose to stay with just one established blend and develop the narrative from there. This strategy of blend maintenance is somewhat analogous to a single, continuously nonmoving camera shot. The three examples that follow illustrate how narrative can be further developed using this discourse strategy.

BLEND MAINTENANCE EXAMPLE 1

Previously, I described how the signer deactivates the hunter blend to establish new grounded blends that indicate the appearance of a deer. This section shows how the signer might provide a similar indication without deactivating the hunter blend. To maintain both blends simultaneously, the signer must produce signs or constructions in a way that leaves crucial mappings intact. This procedure is possible in the following development.

While the hunter blend is still in effect, a bent-V classifier handshape, palm down and facing the signer's right is formed on the left hand and is positioned away from the signer. Then it begins moving toward the right. By itself, the semantics of this classifier handshape restrict the possible referents to chairs and chair-like furniture, seated animates, or four-legged animates. This handshape also needs to receive a particular mapping from the base space. Any of these possible elements could reside in the base space, but in this deer hunt narrative, element **d** *deer* is the logical element. The mapping of element **d** on the classifier results in the grounded blended element |deer|, as shown in figure 7. Note that this mapping is done according to perfectly reasonable assumptions that are based on the narrative context, but the animal that appears could possibly turn out to be not a deer but a bear. Given this possibility, the mapping is thus made provisionally until it is confirmed by further narration.

The establishment of the deer blend and the information within it contributes to the development of the narrative. The hunter blend in which the other parts of the signer's body participate also makes its own contribution. The signer intends to demonstrate the hunter's reaction to the appearance of the deer; thus, he makes a slight modification. While the head position, eye gaze, posture, and right hand remain in place, the facial expression changes to one of recognition combined with continued determination. Because the mappings involved in this blend remain intact, the audience sees that the |hunter| continues to aim his |rifle|, making an appropriate expression as he sees the |deer|.

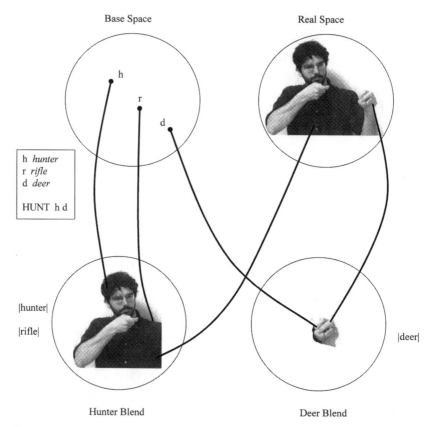

Base Space

Real Space

h

r

d

h *hunter*
r *rifle*
d *deer*

HUNT h d

|hunter|

|rifle|

|deer|

Hunter Blend

Deer Blend

Figure 7.

How does the signer's modification of the classifier predicate (i.e., forming a new classifier predicate with the left hand) affect the hunter blend? Interestingly, no corresponding conceptual change is made to the blend. The audience does not interpret the left hand's movement to its new location as being made within the hunter blend. The movement is made not quite deliberately but in quick fashion. Had the left hand moved in the deliberate manner typically executed in constructed action, the motion would likely be interpreted as being made by the |hunter|. As the left hand moves to the new location, it becomes involved in the construction of the deer blend. When it arrives at the new location, its motions are understood to pertain only to the |deer|.

What about the |hunter|'s left hand? Because all mappings are intact and the only change made in the blend is signaled by the facial expression, the audience understands that the |hunter|'s hand has never left the |rifle|. Although some parts of the |hunter| are visible and other parts are not, all parts of the |hunter| have equal conceptual presence. Conceptual presence does not require full visibility.

The analysis of multiple grounded blends proposed above is further supported by the contrast between physical distance of the left hand from the signer and the conceptual distance between the |hunter| and |deer|. Despite the left hand's proximity to the signer, the visible |deer| is actually understood as being at a location much farther from the |hunter|. This interpretation is based on the following. First, the |hunter|'s eye gaze is not directed to the visible blended element |deer|, but it gazes at a distant location on the |hunter|'s left. This more distant gaze locates the |deer|'s true position relative to the |hunter|. The second cue is the |hunter|'s reaction, which is consistent with the implied distance between |hunter| and |deer|. Had the signer intended for the |deer| to materialize right in front of the |hunter|, he or she would have demonstrated a more appropriate reaction on the part of the |hunter|, perhaps startle or surprise. Yet the |hunter| remains in a fixed position, and his expression is for the most part unflinching.

The preceding discussion illustrates that, when developing narratives, signers have the option of either deactivating or maintaining established grounded blends. Blend deactivation may be followed immediately by a distinct blend or by regular, nonblend narration. Blend maintenance provides further details to the established blend, and it also provides the opportunity to establish a new, simultaneous blend. Therefore, deciding on how to further the narrative is often a strategic matter. Each different strategy has its own effect on the narrative and its flow. Contrast between the effect of "jumping between shots" in the sequencing of grounded blends and the "long shot" in blend. The former quickly alternates between foregrounding the |hunter| and foregrounding the |deer|. Blend maintenance continually foregrounds the |hunter|, and this approach fosters a continued sense of the hunter's deep concentration and determination within the narrative. This sense would be diminished if the strategy of sequencing blends were adopted instead.

BLEND MAINTENANCE EXAMPLE 2

This section examines further development of the narrative through continued grounded blend maintenance. Here, the signer describes the hunter following the deer with his aimed rifle and being pleased at the deer's appearance. Immediately after the deer blend is established, the signer moves the bent-V handshape toward the right. The signer's torso rotates in parallel to the bent-V handshape. All the mappings described in the previous section remain intact, so the visible blended elements |hunter| and |deer| continue to exist. The movement of the bent-V handshape is interpreted as the movement of the |deer|. The rotation of the signer's torso is understood to be the movement of the |hunter|. Because the head and torso move in parallel with the left hand and given the body parts' conceptual status in their respective blends, the audience understands that the |hunter| is following the movement of the |deer|. The |hunter|'s eyes remain, again, not on the visible |deer| but on its implied location, which is much farther from the |hunter|. The |hunter|'s face continues to have a determined expression. Thus, the overall picture the audience sees is the |deer| making its way forward as the |hunter| attentively follows it with his aimed rifle.

As the signer moves his or her left hand and torso, the signer's right hand no longer forms the X classifier handshape but now forms a 5 handshape. The signer moves it to his or her chest to produce the sign FINE! Possible English translations of this sign would include "All right!", "Great!", "Just what I wanted!" This expression confirms that the animal that appeared is indeed a deer.

The right hand, which until now was understood to be the |hunter|'s right hand, is no longer part of the hunter blend. The signer provides no cues to indicate that the |hunter| is signing FINE! If the signer intended for the |hunter| to sign FINE!, he or she would need to make adjustments required by the properties of the blended elements. A real-life scenario will illustrate why adjustments are necessary. A person who is aiming a real rifle with two hands first would have to move his or her trigger finger away from the trigger before being able to sign FINE! Then the person would have to place the 5 handshape with the thumb on his or her chest in a position under the rifle butt while making sure that the shoulder now bears the extra weight formerly shared by the right hand. The signer relating this narrative needs to include similar adjustments if he or she intends the |hunter| to sign FINE! These adjustments would also have to be done in a deliberate manner. In this narrative, however, the right hand moves to the chest in a rapid and nondeliberate manner; therefore, this movement is considered to be transitory and, thus, not part of the hunter blend. The sign FINE! would be seen as a comment by the narrator of the story. This interpretation is reflected in the blended space diagram in figure 8 where the sign FINE! is not included in the hunter blend.

The physical and conceptual changes pertaining to the right hand do not incur corresponding conceptual changes in the hunter blend. Because of the nature of the change and the intact mappings, the audience understands that

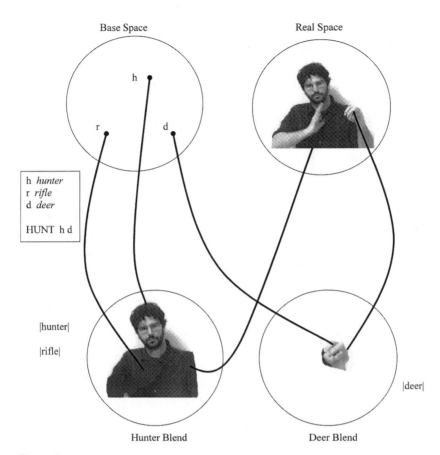

Base Space

Real Space

h

r   d

h *hunter*
r *rifle*
d *deer*

HUNT h d

|hunter|

|rifle|

|deer|

Hunter Blend

Deer Blend

Figure 8.

the |hunter|'s right hand remains at the |rifle|'s trigger. This analysis is similar to the reflections about the changes that pertained to the left hand described in the previous section. Both instances of blend maintenance produce an interesting effect. The two-handed classifier predicate that is produced to establish the hunter blend is now drastically reduced in form to the point where neither hand shows its original configuration or location. Yet the meaning associated with the classifier predicate has not been diminished in any way. Instances such as these do not appear possible without prior establishment of the blend and its maintenance. Indeed, the form produced by the signer in Real Space cannot be signed outside of the hunter blend. Only when the hunter blend is activated is it possible to produce this form.

An instance that follows this narrative development provides further evidence that the |hunter|'s hands never left the |rifle|. As soon as FINE! is produced, the torso ceases its rotation, and both hands return to the respective hand configurations displayed when the hunter blend was established. This change deactivates the deer blend, and the |hunter|'s hands are once again visible. Importantly, the classifier handshapes are now located several degrees away from their initial locations, as if the hands had maintained their respective original positions in relation to the body during the torso's rotation. In this way, the continuity of the hunter blend is preserved. The |hunter|'s hands are where they should be, holding the rifle at a position arrived at through the |hunter|'s torso rotation.

The effectiveness of blend maintenance can be briefly illustrated by the following alternative strategy. As the signer completely deactivates the hunter blend and signs that the hunter is pleased at the appearance of the deer, the signer returns to the neutral posture he or she assumed as narrator. Depending on what follows, this deactivation may or may not disrupt the narrative flow. If the signer does nothing else but immediately reactivate the hunter blend, the deactivation is likely to be judged as disruptive, rendering the narrative less effective.

BLEND MAINTENANCE EXAMPLE 3

This section examines another example of blend maintenance involving a plain verb. Suppose the signer wishes to convey that the hunter does not shoot immediately but waits instead. One possible sign to communicate this delay is WAIT. The citation form of WAIT, shown in figure 9, is a two-handed plain verb, that is, a verb that does not use space. WAIT is not the same as the related imperative YOU-WAIT, which can be produced anywhere in space toward a real or conceived recipient. In contrast, the location of WAIT is quite fixed directly in front of the signer's chest.

Figure 9.

However, in the narrative, WAIT is produced at a location radically different from its citation-form location. As shown in figure 10, the form used is one-handed and is produced near the signer's chin. What is interesting is that, if this form is produced in isolation, signers judge it to be ungrammatical and incomprehensible. When used in an appropriate context, however, this form becomes grammatical and readily understood. As shown in figure 10, this use is possible when a grounded blend such as the hunter blend has been previously established. The grammaticality of the noncitation-form sign WAIT depends on the continued activation of the grounded blend.

In this example, the hunter blend is active, with both |hunter|'s hands on the |rifle|. The signer then proceeds to sign WAIT by forming the 5 handshape and wiggling the fingers, as shown in figure 10. No other changes are made with the right hand. The analysis of this sign production is similar to the one made previously with respect to the role of FINE! in the blend construction. One cannot interpret that the |hunter| is signing WAIT because, if the |hunter|'s right hand were producing the sign, it would coincide with the location of the |rifle| trigger. Among other properties, the |hunter|'s hand and |rifle| also inherit the quality of solidness that individuals and rifles have, that is, they have solid mass that cannot be easily penetrated. Given this property of the blended elements, the |hunter| would have to move his right hand away from the trigger if he were to sign WAIT. This movement would also need to be executed in a deliberate manner.

Because the right hand does not move from its location, one would most likely not interpret that the |hunter| is signing WAIT. The correct interpretation is that the |hunter|'s right hand has made no motion. The signer's action with the right hand causes it to be no longer part of the hunter

Figure 10.

blend. Because all mappings remain in effect, the |hunter| continues to exist albeit a little less visibly. Figure 11 demonstrates the intact mappings involving the base space and Real Space. The sign WAIT appears faded within the hunter blend to indicate that it is not part of the blend.

In cases like the above, many signers prefer to maintain the blend rather than deactivate it. Deactivation of the hunter blend involves the signer returning to neutral position, looking at his or her audience, and signing WAIT in its two-handed form at its citation form location, as shown in figure 9. This deactivation disrupts the narrative flow if the signer does nothing else but immediately reassume the posture of the |hunter| and reactivate the hunter blend. In this instance, deactivation is disfavored because it is counterproductive to the signer's desire to dramatize the scene. Thus, blend maintenance is seen to be an efficient discourse strat-

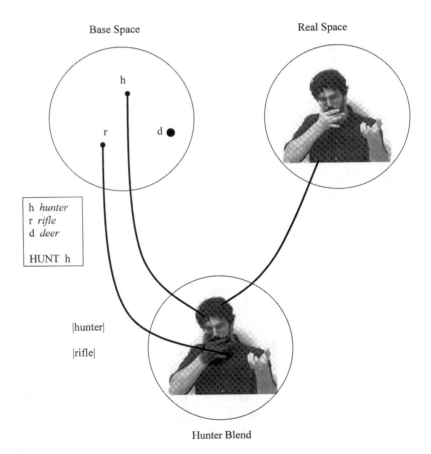

Figure 11.

egy, one that is sometimes necessary for some desired effect that enhances narrative quality.

CONCLUSION

Conceptual entities of the type described in this paper are pervasive in signed language discourse. Conceptual blending theory explains the presence of visible and nonvisible conceptual entities that have great interactive potential. These entities result from the mapping of particular concepts on the body and in space, which brings into being grounded blended elements of rich detail.

Though signers may not be aware of the mechanisms involved, they are aware of the discourse potential that conceptual blending affords them. They may establish single blends that involve their bodies in the blend construction. Signers may also establish simultaneous blends by assigning different body parts to separate blends. These possibilities allow for a repertoire of narrative development strategies. One strategy involves sequencing blends through successive blend deactivation and reactivation. Another strategy, blend maintenance, involves continuous development of a single blend through retention of mappings. The strategies have their respective effects on the narrative and its flow that are analogous to various types of cinematic shots.

The audience's successful interpretation of complex constructions described in this paper is a testimonial to conceptual blending. Conceptual blending can be seen to navigate the audience through the signer's establishment of blends and the constructions that follow. The signer's body parts may have different functions during a single instance of discourse, but partitioning of the elements associated with the body parts minimizes the potential for misinterpretation. Analysis of these and other signed language discourse phenomena stand to gain from further application of conceptual blending theory.

REFERENCES

Coulson, S. 1996. Menedez Brothers Virus: Blended spaces and internet humor. In *Conceptual structure, discourse and language*, ed. A. Goldberg, 67–81. Stanford: CSLI Publications.

———. 2001. *Semantic leaps.* New York: Cambridge University Press.

Fauconnier, G. 1994. *Mental spaces.* New York: Cambridge University Press.

Fauconnier, G., and M. Turner. 1996. Blending as a central process of grammar. In *Conceptual structure, discourse and language,* ed. A. Goldberg, 113–30. Stanford, Calif.: CSLI Publications.

———. 1998. Conceptual integration networks. *Cognitive Science* 22(2): 133–87.

Liddell, S. K. 1995. Real, surrogate, and token space: Grammatical consequences in ASL. In *Language, gesture, and space,* ed. K. Emmorey and J. Reilly, 19–41. Hillsdale, N.J.: Lawrence Erlbaum Associates.

———. 1998. Grounded blends, gestures, and conceptual shifts. *Cognitive Linguistics* 9(3):283–314.

———. 2000. Blended spaces and deixis in sign language discourse. In *Language and gesture,* ed. D. McNeill, 331–57. Cambridge: Cambridge University Press.

Liddell, S. K., and M. Metzger. 1998. Gesture in sign language discourse. *Journal of Pragmatics* 30:657–97.

Metzger, M. 1995. Constructed dialogue and constructed action in American Sign Language. In *Sociolinguistics in deaf communities,* ed. C. Lucas, 255–71. Sociolinguistics in Deaf Communities Series, vol. 1. Washington, D.C.: Gallaudet University Press.

Winston, E. 1991. Spatial referencing and cohesion in an American Sign Language text. *Sign Language Studies* 73:397–410.

———. 1992. Space and involvement in an American Sign Language lecture. In *Expanding horizons: Proceedings of the Twelfth National Convention of the Registry of Interpreters for the Deaf,* ed. J. Plant-Moeller, 93–105. Silver Spring, Md.: RID Publications.

Turn-Taking Mechanisms and Active Participation in Meetings with Deaf and Hearing Participants in Flanders

Mieke Van Herreweghe

If Deaf signers and hearing nonsigners want to attend a joint meeting, communication among them is usually accomplished by means of at least one sign language interpreter.[1] In these "mixed" meetings (with Deaf signers and hearing nonsigners), we generally assume that the presence of a sign language interpreter creates equality of both parties (Deaf and hearing), in other words, that, by means of the sign language interpreter, equal participation of both parties becomes possible. Moreover, as Roy (1993) states,

> To assist outsiders in understanding the practice of the interpreting profession, professional interpreters often describe their role by using metaphors such as "bridge" and "channel" which suggest the link or connection that they make between people who do not speak a common language. Interpreters themselves find it difficult to explain their role without resorting to these conduit metaphors, which then leads to a general perception of interpreters as passive, neutral participants whose job it is to mechanically transmit the content of the source message in the form of the target language. (342)

This concept of the interpreter as the neutral creator of equality leads to what Metzger (1999) calls "The Interpreter's Paradox" (21), or the fact that "[i]nterpreters have expressed the goal of not influencing the form, content, structure, and outcomes of interactive discourse, but the reality is that interpreters, by their very presence, influence the interaction" (23).

The study described in this chapter looked at equal participation of Deaf and hearing participants in a mixed meeting, on the one hand, and the

---

1. It is customary to write *Deaf* with a capital letter *D* for deaf people who regard themselves as members of a linguistic and cultural minority group of sign language users regardless of their degree of hearing loss and to write *deaf* with a small letter *d* when not referring to this linguistic and cultural minority group.

influence of the sign language interpreter on this participation, on the other hand, by observing turn-taking mechanisms used by meeting participants in Flanders. Mixed meetings with one or two sign language interpreters were videotaped, and the turn-taking mechanisms in these mixed meetings were compared to those in all-sign meetings to establish whether participation of Deaf participants in an all-sign meeting is comparable to participation of Deaf participants in a mixed meeting. However, before elaborating on the main issues of this study, some background information on Flanders and signed language in Flanders follows.

BACKGROUND INFORMATION ON FLANDERS AND SIGNED LANGUAGE IN FLANDERS

Flanders is the northern part of Belgium, a small triangular country in Western Europe with its capital, Brussels (which is also the capital of Flanders), situated in the middle of the country. In 1993, Belgium became a federalized monarchy with basically two states (Flanders in the north with about 5,500,000 inhabitants and Wallonia in the south with about 4,500,000 inhabitants) and two official languages: Dutch in Flanders and French in Wallonia.[2] Actually, the situation is more complex because, in addition, the eastern part of Belgium includes a small German-speaking area, and German is the third official language (with about 60,000 speakers), but going into all these political aspects is not necessary. Worth mentioning, though, is that many immigrant workers speaking their various first languages (Turkish, Arabic, etc.) reside in Belgium and that, of course, various signed languages that are not officially recognized are also used.

The Flemish Deaf community is estimated to include approximately 5,000 signed language users. The education of deaf children in Belgium and its neighboring countries was and has continued to be strongly influenced by the resolutions accepted at the Milan Conference in 1880. Deaf children were educated orally, and signs were banned. By the begin-

---

2. The Dutch that is spoken in Flanders is the same language as the Dutch that is spoken in the Netherlands with minor differences (mostly pronunciation differences and, to some extent, lexical and minor grammatical differences). Actually, the two uses can easily be compared to the English that is spoken in the States and the English that is spoken in Britain.

ning of the twentieth century, every major town in Flanders had a Deaf school, and some towns even had two: one for boys and one for girls. Most of the schools were residential schools because of the distances and the way the schools were organized. Pupils went home only during the holidays and, later on, also during the weekends. As a result, regional sign language variants started to develop around every school, so now we are faced with five variants in a state as small as Flanders. In addition, certain differences have evolved in the signs of Deaf men and of Deaf women, although the differences are diminishing rapidly because all the schools have been open to boys and girls for decades. At the moment, Flanders has no standardized sign language, although an ongoing process of spontaneous standardization is occurring primarily because Deaf people from different regions are having more and more contact.

Today, most deaf children are still educated orally, although signs are no longer banned and interest in bilingual-bicultural education is growing rapidly. Consequently, all the adults in Flanders, including deaf and Deaf adults, were educated orally, either in a special education setting or in a mainstream setting (although a small minority of young adults in this group were educated in Total Communication programs using what is called "Nederlands met Gebaren," or "Signed Dutch").

Another important influence on sign language in Flanders is the federalization process that has taken place in Belgium during the last two or three decades. Today, every Belgian, including those who are deaf, belongs to a certain linguistic group. Ironically, Deaf Belgians are also considered Flemish or Walloon; that is, they are regarded as belonging to one of the two linguistic majority groups that speak either Dutch or French, regardless of the signed language they may use or the linguistic minority group to which they might belong. These classifications have major consequences in daily life that range from the choice of the school to which Deaf children are sent (especially in Brussels, which is supposed to be bilingual—Dutch and French—and which has Flemish schools and Walloon schools, etc.) to determinations of whether these children are entitled to a free hearing aid or whether and for how many hours they can get a sign language interpreter. The federalization was a fact in 1993, but this current situation was, of course, the result of a long process. The national Deaf federation, NAVEKADOS, had already split into a Flemish and a Walloon federation in the seventies: *Fevlado (Federatie van Vlaamse Dovenorganisaties,* or the Association of Flemish Deaf Organizations) was founded in 1977.[3] As a result, cultural activities have been organized separately since the seventies, and the Flemish and the Walloon Deaf clubs have been subsidized from different sources. Contacts between Flemish and Walloon Deaf people have become less and less frequent, and this separation has, of course, had its effect on the development of the signed languages in both communities, which seem to be deviating from each other as they are going through separate standardization processes.

In short, up until about fifteen years ago, people were usually signing, talking, and writing about Belgian Sign Language. Now, many Deaf people feel intuitively that the signed language used in Flanders is very different from the one used in the Netherlands (even though the two hearing communities speak the same language, Dutch) but that it is closer to the signed language used in Wallonia (although the Walloon hearing community speaks French). Right now, not enough linguistic evidence has been collected to know whether the differences between Flanders and Wallonia are big enough to allow talk about two different signed languages. Hence, as a good Belgian compromise, the term *Flemish Belgian Sign Language* was used in recent years for the signed language variants used in Flanders. However, because of the split of the national Deaf federation into two regional federations, the fewer and fewer contacts among both organizations and their members, and the separate standardization processes, most Deaf people in Flanders prefer to talk about Flemish Sign Language. This term is also the term that was adopted by Fevlado at its last annual general meeting (AGM) in October 2000. At that AGM, the participants were asked to vote for either the term *Flemish Sign Language* or the term *Flemish Belgian Sign Language*. The first option was nearly unanimously elected. Even though this choice is obviously more politically than linguistically motivated, I want to respect the opinion of the Flemish Deaf Association and its members and will talk about Flemish Sign Language from now on (although, at this point, it is not quite clear whether Deaf people growing

---

3. The Deaf clubs are among the oldest societies in Belgium, and every major town in Flanders has a Deaf club, but many smaller towns also have one, so in total, Flanders has about 25–30 Deaf clubs. Several of them have already celebrated their one hundredth anniversary, for example, the club in Ghent (founded in 1860), the one in Sint-Niklaas (1896), and the one in Aalst (1898). The Belgian Deaf clubs (the Flemish and the Walloon clubs) decided to form a national federation in 1936 and founded NAVEKADOS (the "National Federation of Catholic Deaf-Mutes").

up and living in Brussels are very happy with this development and what Deaf people in Wallonia think of this development).[4] Consequently, in the remainder of this chapter, I will use the term *Flemish Sign Language.*

THE DATA

In May and June 2000, I videotaped the following types of meetings:

- A meeting with parents of deaf children and some professionals at the school of their children, with four Deaf parents, four hearing parents, one hearing chairperson (an educational psychologist), one partially hearing cochairperson (a psychologist), two interpreters, and several hearing professionals (who worked with the children and who only observed the meeting but did not really participate)—This mix of participants was esteemed to be ideal for equal participation. Both chairpersons were well acquainted with Deaf culture (the hearing chairperson actually also has a degree in sign language interpretation), and there were two interpreters, one interpreting from Dutch into Flemish Sign Language (henceforth called the voice-to-sign interpreter) and one interpreting from Flemish Sign Language into Dutch (henceforth called the sign-to-voice interpreter).
- A staff meeting of the teachers in a sign language interpreter training program, with three Deaf teachers, six hearing teachers, one hearing chairperson, and one interpreter—This mix of participants was esteemed to be less ideal, but still good. There was one interpreter, and although the chairperson was not well acquainted with Deaf culture, the other participants in the meeting were.[5]

4. Some time ago, I asked a couple of Walloon Deaf signers what their language is called. They looked at me in a puzzled way and, after some discussion, came up with the term *Langue des Signes Francophone* ("French-speaking Sign Language"), which seemed extremely odd to me. Officially, the Fédération Francophone des Sourds de Belgique (http://www.ffsb.be/) and its Centre Francophone de la Langue des Signes talk about "la Langue des Signes," or "Sign Language."

5. The chairperson was the head of the whole school of which the sign language interpreter training program is only one of the training programs. She has, however, frequently chaired these staff meetings.

- A meeting of the board of Fevlado with seven culturally Deaf participants.—This mix of participants allowed an all-sign meeting, so no interpreters were present. This all-sign meeting needed to be videotaped and analyzed because no literature was found on turn-taking mechanisms in chaired sign language meetings, contrary to the literature on turn-taking mechanisms in chaired spoken language meetings (see next section).

TURN-TAKING MECHANISMS

Turn-Taking Mechanisms in Spoken Language Conversations

According to Sacks, Schegloff, and Jefferson (1974), a current speaker can select a coparticipant to speak next by producing a turn that includes a sequence-initiating action (a first pair-part) and an addressing device. However, a first pair-part alone does not allocate the next turn to some particular participant. Selecting a next speaker is usually accomplished in one of the following ways (Lerner 1993):

By affiliating a name or other identifying term to a sequence-initiating action

By using gaze direction as an addressing device (i.e., by producing a sequence initiating action and at the same time gazing at a single recipient)

By means of embedded addressing accompanied by gaze direction (i.e., referring to a person with the recipient proterm "you"—thus indicating that a single recipient is being addressed without indicating who is being referred to—while using accompanying gaze direction to make clear who is being addressed)

By means of embedded addressing without gaze (i.e., referring to the person with the recipient proterm (you) when that person is clearly identified from the specifics of the situation and of the participants' identities or from the particularities of content and context)

Note that embedded addressing can be unexpressed or tacit, especially in sequence-subsequent addressing.

The Organization of Turn-Taking in Chaired Spoken Language Meetings

Chaired spoken language meetings, however, generally follow a different pattern. The chairperson has close control of the organization of turn-taking and the allocation of the next turn. Thus, in this pattern, we find "a system of third party designation of next speaker" (Larrue and Trognon 1993, 181), which can be described as follows:

> Firstly, when the current speaker indicates the end of his turn, the chairperson is the one who intervenes by calling upon the next speaker. Secondly, the order of the speakers is dictated by the requests to speak expressed as the meeting progresses. Someone who wishes to speak raises his hand. The chairperson writes the requester's name on the list. He will grant that speaker a turn when all preceding individuals on the list have spoken. (181)

Turn-Taking Mechanisms in Signed Conversations

One of the questions this study addresses is whether the organization of turn-taking in spoken language conversations can be applied equally to the organization of turn-taking in signed language conversations. Baker (1977) looked at a small corpus of conversations between two Deaf signers and concentrated on initiation, continuation, and shift regulators, using a taxonomy devised by Wiener and Devoe (1974).[6] In her study, Baker (1977) distinguished between initiation regulators by the signer and initiation regulators by the addressee. A signer, for instance, can initiate a turn by raising and extending the hand or hands out of rest position, which can then be followed by optional indexing, touching, or waving of a hand in front of the addressee to get his or her attention. When beginning a statement, a signer usually does not look at the addressee (−GAZE), but when asking a question, he or she usually does (+GAZE). The addressee can signal that the signer may initiate a turn by +GAZE or by maintaining his or her own inactivity, that is, by not signing. With respect to shift regulators, again, a distinction can be made between the signer signaling turn yielding and the addressee signaling

6. Continuation regulators will not be discussed here because they are not relevant for this chapter.

turn claiming. The most important turn-yielding signal by the signer is a return to +GAZE that is optionally accompanied by a decrease in signing speed near the termination of the turn, by an optional call for addressee response (e.g., indexing the addressee at the end of the turn), or both. The signer then moves his or her hands to rest position. The addressee can signal turn claiming during the speaker's turn by using the following strategies:

a. Optional increase in size and quantity of head-nodding, often accompanied by a concurrent increase in size and quantity of indexing the speaker

b. Optional switch to palm$_a$ (i.e., palm up with heel raised higher than fingertips)

c. Movement out of rest position to get speaker's attention—may include indexing, touching, or waving hand in front of speaker

d. Switching to −GAZE when speaker is +GAZE—may include postural shift, looking up (as if thinking while preparing to sign), facial signaling of forthcoming question, disagreement, etc.

e. Initiating turn (interrupting) and repeating first few signs until speaker is +GAZE and has yielded the floor or until speaker suppresses addressee's turn-claim (Baker 1977, 219)

Because Baker (1977) looked at dyadic conversations, focusing on the selection of the next speaker or on the allocation of the next turn was not necessary. However, her analysis of speaker-initiated turns is to some extent comparable to what happens when a speaker self-selects in a multiparty conversation or in a meeting, as will become clear in the following section.

Turn-Taking Mechanisms in a Mixed Conversation with a Sign Language Interpreter

Turn-taking mechanisms in a mixed conversation with a sign language interpreter also follow a different pattern. Roy (1989, 1993) analyzed a videotaped meeting that occurred involving a professor, a doctoral student, and an interpreter and focused on, among other things, the interpreter's role in simultaneous talk or overlap. She claims that interpreters have four options in the case of overlap:

(1) The interpreter can stop one or both speakers and, in that way, halt the turn of one speaker, allowing the other speaker to continue. If the

interpreter stops both speakers, it is possible that one of the primary speakers will decide who talks next, or the interpreter may make that decision. (2) The interpreter can momentarily ignore one speaker's overlapping talk, hold (in memory) the segment of talk from that speaker, continue interpreting the other speaker, and then produce the "held" talk immediately following the end of the other speaker's turn. . . . (3) The interpreter can ignore the overlapping talk completely. (4) The interpreter can momentarily ignore the overlapping talk, and upon finishing the interpretation of one speaker, offer a turn to the other primary speaker, or indicate in some way that a turn was attempted. (Roy 1993, 350)

In Roy's study, whatever the interpreter chose to do, ultimately, it was the interpreter who resolved turn-taking problems created by overlap, and thus, it was the interpreter who made a decision: "In particular, the interpreter recognized overlap quickly, and made sociolinguistic choices to resolve overlap by deciding and allocating who would get the next turn" (Roy 1993, 360). Thus, the interpreter is not a neutral conduit but has an active role "in managing the intercultural event of interpreting" (Roy 1993, 341).

RESULTS AND DISCUSSION

Turn-Taking Mechanisms in All-Sign Meetings

Because I found no literature on turn-taking mechanisms in all-sign chaired meetings, I decided to videotape that kind of a meeting and analyze it. The following section describes some specific mechanisms that were found in a two-hour meeting of the board of Fevlado, with seven Deaf participants, all using Flemish Sign Language. This meeting was a regular board meeting that is held about every month, and no special issues were addressed that could have made this board meeting different from others.

In looking at how the next turn can be allocated in this type of meeting, two major and striking differences appeared that contrasted with usual descriptions of spoken language multiparty conversations. First, in spoken language conversations, one of the most important means of allocating the next turn to someone is by affiliating a name or other identifying term to a sequence-initiating action—which was not done at all in the two-hour all-sign meeting. Participants in the all-sign meeting never used names or other identifying terms when they were addressing someone to allocate the next turn to that person. Names or other identifying terms were used when talking about someone but never as an addressing device. Second, embedded addressing without eye gaze, another means of allocating the next turn in spoken language conversations, was never done in the all-sign meeting. On the contrary, eye gaze proved to be an extremely important and powerful regulator that a current speaker used to select the next speaker.

The ways in which a speaker could self-select in the all-sign meeting were very similar to some of the signals described by Baker (1977) as addressees' turn-claiming regulators. In particular, actions such as waving a hand, indexing, lightly touching the current speaker on the arm, and tapping the table were frequently used by participants who wanted to self-select as next speaker.[7] A variant of this behavior, which did not occur all that often and which was not described by Baker (1977), was stretching out a 5 classifier handshape with the palm away from the speaker and the fingers up, just above the table. This action was used in only one particular context: A speaker gave the floor to another speaker but, at the same time, indicated that he wanted the floor back by stretching out this 5 classifier handshape all through the next speaker's turn. Another variant, again not used very often, ran as follows: A signaled to B (the person sitting next to the current speaker) that B was to warn the current speaker that A wants the next turn. This action was not used very often, probably because it is a fairly cumbersome method involving a third party. It was used only when the self-selecting speaker thought the current speaker had not noticed that he or she wanted the next turn, and even then, it was used only after waving a hand, tapping the table, or so forth was not successful.

One important difference between self-selection in a dyadic conversation and self-selection in a multiparty conversation, however, is that whoever self-selects as next speaker in a multiparty conversation will get the floor only when the current speaker looks at him or her rather than at any of the other participants. So self-selection in a multiparty conversation is

7. Interestingly, the way in which men and women waved in this all-sign meeting indicated an apparent gender difference. The men each raised one hand high up in the air, well above their heads. The women each raised a hand until it was almost next to their heads (unless they really wanted the floor in which case they raised the hand higher). Further research will have to establish whether this variation is a genuine gender difference or whether it was typical only of the people attending this meeting. Tapping the table was not mentioned by Baker (1977).

never pure self-selection because the current speaker still has the power to allocate the next turn by means of eye gaze. Frequently during the two-hour meeting, more than one person wanted to claim a turn (i.e., self-select) at the same time, and each of them signaled this intention by means of waving a hand (the most frequently used signal by far). Thus, while the current speaker was still holding the floor, two or three participants were each waving a hand, each signaling that he or she was self-selecting, but the current speaker, using gaze direction, allocated the next turn to only one of these participants. So the current speaker—and not the chairperson—had the power to select the next speaker even when more than one participant were self-selecting. This situation is obviously different from a multiparty spoken language conversation where the power of the current speaker is not that strong.

Also striking in this meeting was that the process to allocate the next turn was totally different from the system of third-party designation of next speaker, as described by Larrue and Trognon (1993) when analyzing chaired spoken language meetings. In their analysis, allocation of the next turn was done nearly exclusively by the chairperson. In the two-hour, all-sign meeting that I analyzed, allocation by the chairperson happened only once, and even then, it occurred as part of an extremely confusing turn-allocation sequence (see example 1).

EXAMPLE I.

is signing, and M. tries to get the next turn. This endeavor proves quite difcult, however, as can be seen in the transcript:[8]

```
:      (signing)[9]——————————————————————————————
hair:  (waving hand)[10]____YES I KNOW (waves____points at M., waves)_____
```

8. The customary musical-score format will be used in the transcriptions of multiparty conversations in this study: "The musical-score format of transcription is one way of representing the simultaneous and overlapping nature of interactive discourse. As described by Ehlich (1993), the musical-score format allows the sequence of events to unfold from left to right on a horizontal line, while the list of participants occurring from top to bottom allow each person's utterance to be captured within a single moment of overlap" (44).

9. Because what J. is signing does not really matter in this example, I chose not to transcribe his utterances for the sake of clarity. However, the dotted line indicates that he is signing, with his eye gaze directed at G.

10. The line indicates that the waving is being continued.

M.:	(raises hand)_____
J.:	————————————
Chair:	(waves with other hand)____EXISTS I KNOW speak (points at M.)
M.:	NO NO ADD (raises finger)_____
G.:	(points at chair, taps M.'s leg)[11] BEST LOOK-AT CHAIR

M.:   (starts signing)

Example 1 shows that M. is trying to get the floor but that J. is not willing to yield. In the end, the chairperson has to intervene; however, only when G. also intervenes, telling M. that she had better look at the chairperson to see what he has to say, does the chairperson get the next turn (after which he allocates the next turn to M.). G.'s intervention is noteworthy because, in this fragment, eye gaze is extremely important. J. keeps looking at G. (the previous speaker) and nearly refuses—although *refuse* may be too strong a word—to look at the chairperson, who wants to intervene but cannot. Only when G. (who sits next to the chairperson) notices that the chairperson wants to say something does he look away from J., which is the point when the chairperson gets the floor and subsequently allocates the next turn to M.

As has been said before, except for this one example, allocation of the next turn in the all-sign meeting was done by the current speaker, not by the chairperson. Of course, whether this behavior is typical only of Fevlado board meetings or whether this behavior is a general characteristic of all-sign meetings is not clear. More research is needed to corroborate this finding.

Turn-Taking Mechanisms in Mixed Meetings with One or Two Sign Language Interpreters

TURN ALLOCATION AND OVERLAP

The system of turn allocation in all-sign meetings, as described above, is completely different from the system that is used in a mixed meeting with one or two sign language interpreters. One major difference is caused by a far more restricted use of gaze direction in mixed meetings. A striking observation was that all the hearing participants (except for the interpreters) looked at who was talking, whether Deaf or hearing, whereas the

11. He taps her leg because she was not looking at him but at J., who was still signing.

Deaf participants looked at the interpreter. Consequently, the Deaf participants had no control over the organization of turn-taking and the allocation of the next turn because their gaze direction necessarily was restricted to the interpreter, which was a completely different pattern from what occurred during all-sign meetings.

For the hearing participants, however, the situation was not all that different from chaired spoken language meetings because, in those meetings, the chairperson is in charge and organizes the allocations of the next turn. In chaired meetings with a sign language interpreter, this control necessarily is quite tight because the interpreter can interpret for only one person at a time; thus, only one person at a time can talk. One can imagine that, in mixed meetings led by a chairperson who knows nothing about the dynamics of interpretation, turn allocation can go completely wrong. However, both of the mixed meetings that were analyzed for this article were chaired by people who were well acquainted with these dynamics. In these chaired mixed meetings, the participants had to signal the chairperson when they wanted the floor. Consequently, the Deaf participants had to break eye contact with the sign language interpreter and seek eye contact with the chairperson, as in example 2 (from the meeting with two interpreters).[12]

EXAMPLE 2.[13]

R. (Deaf parent) asks for the floor by looking away from the voice-to-sign interpreter—who stands next to and slightly in front of the chairperson—and by looking at the chairperson while slightly raising a hand. The chairperson has seen this signal and acknowledges it to R. by means of

12. In the meeting with two interpreters, the Deaf participants could have also sought eye contact with the sign-to-voice interpreter so she could signal to the chairperson that one of the Deaf parents wanted the next turn, but this approach never happened during the entire meeting. I assume this strategy was not used because the Deaf parents knew that the chairperson could understand Flemish Sign Language. They probably preferred to signal directly to him that they wanted the floor rather than indirectly by means of the sign-to-voice interpreter. It would be interesting to see what happens in a meeting with a chairperson who does not understand Flemish Sign Language.

13. I chose not to transcribe this example and some of the other example interactions in a musical-score format because they would become extremely cumbersome and probably very confusing because of the complex exchange of eye gazes. For the sake of clarity, I chose to give a prose description.

a short nod and the OK sign, so R. looks back at the voice-to-sign inter-preter. The current speaker (hearing) continues for a while, then stops, and immediately, the chairperson nods at R. to give him the floor. R. sees this signal in his peripheral vision field while he is still looking at the voice-to-sign interpreter. However, at this point, the voice-to-sign interpreter is still interpreting (her last sign is produced just after the chairperson nods at R.). R. sees the voice-to-sign interpreter stop, checks whether the cur-rent (hearing) speaker has also stopped, then looks again at the chair-person and at the current speaker, raises his hand while looking at the sign-to-voice interpreter—(who sits next to her colleague), and starts signing. When he raises his hand, the sign-to-voice-interpreter says his name.

In example 2, R. seems confused by the fact that he got the floor from the chairperson while the voice-to-sign interpreter was still signing. Thus, he does all the checking. After he is convinced that the current speaker has stopped talking and after having checked with the chairperson, he signals to the sign-to-voice interpreter by raising his hand that he is going to start. All of this checking, of course, takes time, so a fairly long pause occurs between the hearing speaker's last utterance and R.'s first.

Signaling to the chairperson that one wants the floor can sometimes be quite difficult, especially when the chairperson has not noticed it, as in example 3 (from the meeting with two interpreters).

EXAMPLE 3.

The current speaker (hearing) stops talking. L. (one of the Deaf parents) raises his hand while looking at the chairperson, but the chairperson has not seen this signal. The voice-to-sign interpreter looks at the sign-to-voice interpreter, but she doesn't say anything. L. raises his hand again, and the voice-to-sign interpreter points at the sign-to-voice interpreter, but again, she does not react. At this point, the chairperson points to and looks at the next speaker (hearing) who starts with "ehm." The voice-to-sign inter-preter then looks at the chairperson (who is sitting slightly behind her) to find out whether he has seen that L. had indicated that he wanted the floor, pointing at L. while looking at the chairperson. The chairperson sud-denly realizes his mistake, looks at L., and apologizes by saying "Oh, sorry" (which is interpreted by the voice-to-sign interpreter). The chair-person then signs WAIT toward the hearing parent (without saying anything, and it is not voiced by the interpreter[14]) and gives the floor to L. by pointing at him and nodding at him. L. then shifts his eye gaze from the chairperson to the voice-to-sign interpreter. The voice-to-sign interpreter, who has eye contact with L., points at the sign-to-voice interpreter and signs VOICE to signal that L. has to look at the other interpreter because she will interpret what he signs into spoken Dutch.

In this example, both the chairperson and the sign-to-voice interpreter had not noticed that L. had asked for the floor. Fortunately, the voice-to-sign interpreter had noticed, so through her intervention, the chairperson could correct this misallocation and give L. the next turn. When something similar happened with the hearing participants (i.e., that the chairperson had not seen their signaling to ask for the floor), they simply supported their signaling by using their voice, and the chairperson immediately reacted to the sound. The Deaf participants, in contrast, depend on the interpreters when the chairperson has missed their signaling.[15]

This whole process of signaling is even more difficult when only one interpreter is present. In example 4, taken from the meeting with only one interpreter, the chairperson is talking, and the interpreter is interpreting her statements into Flemish Sign Language.[16] At the same time, one of the Deaf participants has signaled, wanting to say something, but the chairperson hasn't seen the signal, and the interpreter cannot interpret that signal while signing the chairperson's statements at the same time.

14. It is very strange that the hearing chairperson would use a sign toward the hearing parents (some of them know a bit of Flemish Sign Language, but some of them don't). Apparently, this signing was just a result of a bilingual person being confronted with both languages that he or she knows; one sometimes gets confused and addresses people in the wrong language. The sign-to-voice interpreter couldn't have interpreted this signing because she was looking at the Deaf parents and was sitting with her back to the chairperson (who was supposed to talk, not sign).

15. None of the Deaf parents ever used their voices during the meeting.

16. These and subsequent conversations were, of course, in Dutch, but for the sake of clarity in the examples, I decided to translate them into English.

EXAMPLE 4.[17]

Chair: . . . but I would also like with them, well, ask what it was like and how they
W. (Deaf teacher):   (waves his hand
Inter.:   BUT   ALSO   LIKE   HOW   FEEL   HOW   THEY

Chair: themselves see it in the training program. That is . . . very short. Now obviously
W.:   (drops his hand, raises his finger)   ONLY   (waves his hand
Inter.:   LOOK-AT-IT   IN   TRAINING PROGRAM   VERY SHORT

Chair: evaluation, eh, a talk
W.:   ONLY WE-TWO
Inter.: NOW Is that individually W. asks, only you and and us, oh yes, so then
W.:   INTERPRETER NOT NECESSARY ME
Inter.: I don't need an interpreter.

Clearly, in this case of overlap, the interpreter decides to halt the turn
of the chairperson and to allow the Deaf teacher to start a turn. (Compare
Roy's first option: "The interpreter can stop one or both speakers and, in
that way, halt the turn of one speaker, allowing the other speaker to continue" [1993, 350].) The chairperson's turn, which the interpreter interrupted, started with "Now . . .", which often signals a transition-relevant
moment. The interpreter recognized the utterance as this kind of signal and
decided to interrupt the chairperson. So at this point, the interpreter is the
one who allocates the next turn and the one who manages the organization of turn taking.

In example 5 (taken from the same meeting as example 4), the interpreter clearly is confused and does not know whether to interpret from sign
to voice or from voice to sign. She apparently decides to interpret from sign
to voice, probably because the Deaf person had started first and she had
focused on what he was signing, but this decision required her to interrupt
the chairperson.

17. This sequence is about the fact that the chairperson, who is also the head
of the school, wants an evaluation talk with each of the teachers at the end of the
school year.

EXAMPLE 5.

W. (Deaf teacher):   SHALL SEE WHO SUPPORT WORKING GROUP RESPONSIBLE

W.:   COORDINATION ETC. WORKING GROUP SEE WHO SUPPORT
Chair:[1]   Will you later on make an appointment for that, eh very

W.:   COORDINATE
Chair: concretely, or
Inter.: W. also says, sorry, W. also says that in that group there needs to be a form of

Inter.: support, that there needs to be a sort of coordinator of the working group.

When the chairperson forgets about his or her role as coordinator of the meeting and forgets to allocate the next turn, turn taking can become completely disrupted. Either people start talking at the same time and the interpreter is at a loss or (and this situation occurs especially when only one interpreter is present) people are speaking and signing at the same time and the signing is not being interpreted. Because the interpreter can interpret for only one person at a time, she cannot deal with overlap. Example 6 illustrates the first result described above (from the meeting with two interpreters).

EXAMPLE 6.

A hearing parent (K.) and the cochairperson (J.) are talking at the same time, so the voice-to-sign interpreter, hearing both voices, chooses to interpret the cochairperson. When the cochairperson stops talking, two hearing parents respond to him at the same time. The voice-to-sign interpreter then signs to the Deaf participants that she cannot interpret, that they are all talking at the same time. The chairperson sees what the interpreter is signing, also understands her signing, intervenes, and indirectly asks the two hearing parents to stop talking by saying to the cochairperson, "Please, J., hold on, this cannot be interpreted that way, it's also eh, very annoying in this room when people are all talking at the same time, sorry" (pause in which R. [Deaf parent] signs "Wait, I can't follow" and F. [Deaf parent] signs "I don't understand it").[19] The chair-

18. The chairperson hadn't seen that W. was signing.
19. The chairperson's utterances were not interpreted into sign language. When the chair says "K.," the voice-to-sign interpreter points at K. and resumes interpreting.

person then says, "OK we . . . we were busy here, K. and J., I interrupted you . . .", and K. continues talking.

This sequence shows that the voice-to-sign interpreter did not really know how to deal with the overlap. She first tries to interpret from one speaker (the cochairperson, J.), ignoring the other speaker (K.). Maybe she thought that, after having finished interpreting what the cochairperson said, she could interpret consecutively what K. had said. This approach would have corresponded with Roy's second option: "The interpreter can momentarily ignore one speaker's overlapping talk, hold (in memory) the segment of talk from that speaker, continue interpreting the other speaker, and then produce the 'held' talk immediately following the end of the other speaker's turn" (1993, 350). However, after J.'s utterances, two hearing parents immediately respond (while K. is still talking), and then the interpreter realizes that she cannot deal with all the overlapping talk. She chooses not to warn the chairperson, however, but, instead, signs to the Deaf participants that she cannot interpret, that several participants are all talking at the same time. Two of the Deaf participants react by signing that they don't understand, but these reactions are not interpreted by the sign-to-voice interpreter, probably because the two Deaf participants had made eye contact with the chairperson, who can understand Flemish Sign Language. The sign-to-voice interpreter also knew the cochairperson's sign skills and probably decided that this message was one for the chairperson only and that she did not have to interpret it because he could understand Flemish Sign Language. At this point, the chairperson makes everybody stop and allocates the next turn to K.

In this scenario, neither interpreter chose to manage the organization of turn-taking. One did not say anything, and the other simply announced that she could not do her job. They obviously chose not to resolve the problem caused by overlap but wanted other people (the Deaf participants, the chairperson) to resolve the problem. Interestingly, this option was not mentioned by Roy (1993), probably because this type of simultaneous talk is possible in multiparty conversations but not in dyadic conversations (such as the one she studied).

In the meeting with one interpreter, many examples could be found of problems caused by overlap (see examples 7, 8, 9, 10). In each instance, the interpreter was still interpreting (mostly from voice-to-sign) when one of the participants (usually one of the Deaf teachers) self-selected. The interpreter resolved these instances of overlap by simply ignoring the overlapping talk and by not interpreting what the self-selected person said or signed. This approach corresponds with Roy's third option: "The interpreter can ignore the overlapping talk completely" (1993, 350), which results in loss.

EXAMPLE 7.

G. (Deaf teacher) signs "ONE SOCKET THERE ONE THERE ONE" followed by W. (Deaf teacher) signing "THERE ONE MULTIPLE-SOCKET IN-CABINET THERE," none of which was interpreted because the interpreter was still interpreting from voice to sign.

EXAMPLE 8.

H. (Deaf teacher) waves and signs HAS-TO KNOW WHAT TO-CHOOSE SORRY. H. had suddenly realized that the interpreter was still interpreting into Flemish Sign Language and that the interpreter can't do both, so H. stops signing and does not take the floor. H. does not volunteer this comment again later, either.

EXAMPLE 9.

Chair: Can you start working on the group, because that seems ehm if it is possible . . . (At the same time, W. [Deaf teacher] waves, points at M. [one of the hearing teachers] and signs)

_____t

SAY WORKING GROUP DEAF TEACHERS WOULD-LIKE THIS MONTH TO-BEGIN / NO CLASS / HOLIDAY.

(What W. signed was not interpreted because the interpreter had not finished interpreting from voice to sign, but apparently W. was not aware of that because, a little bit further in the meeting, he quite obviously assumes that the others (Deaf and hearing) have taken account of his remark.)

EXAMPLE 10.

Chair: The second year . . . the expected number of students is 35, it may be a little less or a little more, ehm, the expected number is 35 anyway. I would suggest let us try there also to work with two groups . . . I see . . . 35 . . . (When she says "try," W. [Deaf teacher]—who will be the second-year teacher, so it is his class she is talking about—signs)

BIG GROUP SMALL GROUP SMALL GROUP BIG GROUP I CANNOT

(Again this statement was not interpreted because the interpreter was still busy interpreting from voice to sign.)

SELF SELECTION

A couple of times, speakers self-selected, so the next turn was not allocated by the chairperson in those cases. Signers successfully self-selected only when the person currently speaking or signing directed his or her eye gaze at the potential self-selector and not at the interpreter. Thus, a Deaf person can self-select only when he or she makes eye contact with the current speaker. These instances of self-selection were very similar to the ones found in the all-sign meeting. In all these cases, the gazes of the signers were directed at each other and not at the chairperson or the interpreters. A couple of times in the mixed meeting, the self-selectors suddenly realized that allocation of the next turn is normally done by the chairperson and that, in this type of formal meeting, self-selection is not the norm. So they then checked with the chairperson to see whether they could take the floor. Each time, the chairperson had to take into account that a small time lapse always occurs between what is being signed and the interpretation. He thus had to ask the self-selected signer to wait until the sign-to-voice interpreter had finished (see examples 11 and 12).

EXAMPLE 11.

While signing, R. (Deaf parent) looks at F. (also Deaf parent) and continues to sign. R. then stops signing and looks at F., thus, selecting the next speaker. F. also looks at R. and starts to sign when suddenly it dawns on him that he has to ask permission from the chairperson, so he looks at the chairperson who signs WAIT directly to him. When the sign-to-voice interpreter has stopped, then the chairperson nods so F. can start signing.

EXAMPLE 12.

F. (Deaf parent) is signing and the sign-to-voice interpreter is interpreting his utterances. F. then stops (but the sign-to-voice interpreter has not finished yet) and looks at R. (Deaf parent), thus, selecting him as next speaker. —R. immediately wants to start (signs ALSO, raises finger, looks at chairperson, and waits), but in this case, the voice-to-sign interpreter signs WAIT because the chairperson is writing something. When the chairperson looks up, he also signs WAIT to allow the sign-to-voice interpreter to finish talking.

When a hearing participant self-selected, the interpreter had to indicate the self-selection. In the meeting with two interpreters, the voice-to-sign interpreter usually made this indication, certainly with respect to the chairperson who obviously often self-selected. When the chairperson started talking and the interpreter started interpreting, the interpreter, using her thumb, usually pointed over her shoulder at the chairperson (because he sat slightly behind her). Metzger (1999) calls this indicating an "interpreter-generated utterance" with the function of "source attribution" (101):

In monolingual interactive discourse, when an interlocutor begins an utterance, addressees are generally able to determine that a turn has been initiated and who is the source of that turn, in addition to receiving access to the content of the utterance. How this is accomplished in ASL and English discourse is somewhat different, however. When interpreting between two distinct modalities, information about the occurrence and source of an original utterance might not be accessible to participants without an interpreter-generated contribution. Therefore, for ASL-English interpreters, the rendering of all three parts of an utterance is an important consideration. Because this discourse-relevant information is not directly available to participants who are native to languages conveyed in two different modes, there is the potential for participants to experience confusion regarding who is the original source of a given utterance, or even when another participant begins a turn.

In English monolingual interaction the interlocutors are generally able to hear when someone begins a turn at talk. On the basis of prior exposure to the speaker's voice, the addressee or overhearer can generally identify the speaker (as a familiar person or someone unknown). Similarly, in ASL turns are initiated in part on the basis of eye gaze. When an addressee is not gazing in the direction of an interlocutor who is initiating a turn, the potential addressee is summoned until eye contact is made, allowing the turn to begin.

The interpreters convey this information by generating utterances. These utterances (e.g., a summons or source attribution) provide the information normally accessible in monolingual interaction. Thus, the interpreter-generated contributions can be seen to function in a manner that makes the interpreted interaction similar to monolingual interactive discourse. That is, each participant receives information similar to the information that would be accessible in a monolingual interview. It is important to reiterate that the interpreters did not always provide this information consistently. The issue here is that such contributions seem to represent a similarity to monolingual interaction. Clearly, a difference is that the interpreter has the power to omit information that is, by necessity, always present in monolingual discourse.[20] (Metzger 1999, 159–60)

Just as in Metzger's data (1999), the interpreters in our data also did not always mention source attribution consistently, as shown in example 13.

EXAMPLE 13.

The chairperson allocates the next turn to one of the hearing parents by saying her name. The interpreter, however, does not indicate that the chairperson had said something (i.e., the name of the next speaker), but immediately points at the hearing parent, thus giving the Deaf participants the impression that the hearing parent had self-selected.

Moreover, the interpreter also sometimes completely forgot to indicate who was talking, especially when the next speaker had self-selected (see example 14).

EXAMPLE 14.

Chair: In your family, there actually was some experience, eh (H. [hearing parent] says "yes, so eh," but is not interpreted. The chairperson then continues.)—but nevertheless, still, from the feeling more like we have seen in the first fragment and what actually corresponds with the (H. interjects "yes," without interpretation.) hearing parent in this tape.

H.: (Interpreting occurs with no source indication.) Yes, I want to say that in the case of my nephew it was not hereditary, that it actually was through an accident that he became deaf.

Here, the interpreter interprets what the chairperson says (but not the short back-channeling utterances by the hearing parent) and follows with

20. Just because monolingual discourse consists of three parts—(1) the initiation of a turn, (2) who is the source of that turn, and (3) the content of the utterance—does not warrant calling the information the interpreters provide about the source of the utterance an "interpreter-generated utterance" because it is an essential part of the source language utterance. Nevertheless, I still agree with Metzger's argument in general.

the interpretation of the hearing parent without a pause or an indication of the fact that a different person is speaking. Presumably, the Deaf participants thought that the chairperson was still talking, although after a while, they noticed that the chairperson was not saying anything anymore, and they quickly glanced at where the hearing parents were sitting, probably to find out who was talking. This glancing around occurred, however, after the hearing parent had already talked for some time. When the interpreter did not attribute the source of the utterance, the Deaf participants obviously lost information.

Self-selection by a signer when a hearing person was speaking proved extremely difficult. Self-selection hardly ever occurred across a Deaf-hearing scenario, and if it did, it was problematic. In the meeting with only one interpreter, this kind of self-selection always resulted in loss or overlap, as was shown in examples 7–10. In the meeting with two interpreters, self-selection proved difficult because the interpreters always lagged behind, as can be seen in example 15.[21]

EXAMPLE 15.

Chair: I can hear from your story, R., that it is too simple to think that all Deaf
V—S Inter.:　　(points at chair)　　HEAR R. HEAR　　TOO

Chair:　people ehm would like to have deaf children, right, or don't have any problem
V—S Inter.:　CANNOT SAY ALL DEAF PEOPLE LIKE DEAF CHILDREN
R.:　　　　　　　　　　　　　　　　　NOT-NOT-

Chair:　with that and that all hearing people would have problems with it, right, with the fact that
V–S Inter.:　NO PROBLEM DEAF CHILDREN OTHER-SIDE ALL HEARING
R.:　NOT-NOT-NO-NO-NO　　NOT-NOT-NOT-NOT

Chair:　their children are deaf, right?
V—S Inter.:　PEOPLE PROBLEM DEAF CHILDREN NOT TWO-SIDES
R.:　　　　　　　　　NOT-NOT

Chair:　I also hear in your story
V—S Inter.:　　HEAR

21. Trying to avoid lag time is not a successful strategy. In examining American Sign Language-English interpreters, Cokely (1992) clearly showed that shorter lag times result in a higher number of miscues and, thus, in a lower quality of output.

| S—V Inter.: | | that is not the case, no, no, that is not the case |

Chair: I also hear in your story
V—S Inter.:   I HEAR YOUR STORY

The chairperson is talking, and the voice-to-sign interpreter interprets what he says into Flemish Sign Language. R. immediately self-selects by signing NOT-NOT-NOT- and so forth. R.'s utterances are not immediately interpreted by the sign-to-voice interpreter but are voiced a bit later. She seems to have waited for a while, probably because she did not want to interrupt the chairperson. When the chairperson starts with a second line of thought ("I also hear in your story"), she decides to go ahead and interrupt him, so her voice overlaps with the chairperson's and he has to repair. In an interpreted conversation between a hearing person and a Deaf person, the "interpretational lag" makes it very difficult for the interpreter to know when he or she can interrupt the speaker when the signer has self-selected (who also lags behind because he or she has to wait for the voice-to-sign interpretation).

MAKING SURE EVERYBODY PARTICIPATES

In all-sign meetings, a signer usually checks whether the other participants are looking at him or her. When a signer sees that a person is not looking—because she or he is reading something, for instance—the signer will either tap the table or ask the neighbor to warn the person that conversation has started again. In the mixed meetings, this behavior hardly ever occurred. In fact, quite frequently, a hearing person started talking and the interpreter started interpreting, but one or more Deaf people were not looking at the interpreter (see examples 16 and 17 from the meeting with one interpreter).

EXAMPLE 16.

Chair (interpreted but not shown in transcription): . . . the question is whether we can find a joint date so people who are interested can meet with the architect. It has to be before 15 June. (At this point, three deaf teachers look away from the interpreter; G. and H. start talking to each other, and W. looks in his diary.

Chair: So speed is important. It can be an evening, it can be a Saturday, it can be during the day, it can be at lunchtime. No problem, the architect will adjust. (A long break occurs in which everything is interpreted, but only G. looks at the interpreter.

Chair: Preferably an evening?

H.:   :I FULL, FULL, FULL, FULL. (long pause)
Interpreter: My diary is full.

<pre>   _____wh</pre>
H.:   FIND DURING-THE-DAY SOMETHING I EVENING MUST EVENING
Interpreter: Does it have to be in the evening? I can find something during the day, but evenings are difficult.
(H. had missed out on part of the information because she hadn't looked at the
interpreter, and the chairperson hadn't checked to see that she was watching the
interpreter.)

EXAMPLE 17.

(G. and W. [both Deaf teachers] are not looking at the interpreter.)
Chair: Thursday 29 July. (pause) Who can be present at the info?

A. (hearing teacher): I am free 29 July and 24 August, but between 27 August
and 2 September I am not free. (G. looks up.) So I can't then. (G. looks down
again.)

B. (hearing teacher): But maybe first ehm info how are we gonna do that, how
could we do it best. (G. looks up, but W. keeps looking down for 1.5 minutes.)

(Nobody checked whether the Deaf participants were looking at the interpreter.)

A similar phenomenon can be seen when papers are distributed during
a meeting. When papers were distributed in the all-sign meeting, some time
was given for people to look at them. Afterwards, the person who distributed the papers explained what was written down, showed the relevant
passage to the whole group so everybody knew the passage about which
he or she was talking, and then discussed it. When papers were distributed
in the mixed meetings, no time was given to look at them. The hearing participants listened to the explanations and looked at the papers at the same
time. However, the Deaf participants had to choose between looking at the
paper or looking at the interpreter. In one instance during the meeting with
one interpreter, one of the Deaf participants read some papers that had just
been distributed during the entire explanation by the chairperson, which
lasted for several minutes. Nobody warned the Deaf person that he had

to look at the interpreter. During this same situation, another Deaf participant actually held up the paper so she could try to look at the paper and at the interpreter at the same time. Regardless, the Deaf participants were not given sufficient time to first read the papers and then look at the explanations. Moreover, the relevant passages were not shown to the Deaf participants.

The question is whether the interpreter should have pointed out that one or more of the Deaf participants were not looking at her. In the all-sign meeting, the Deaf participants—usually the signer who has the floor—make sure that everybody is looking at whoever is signing. If the interpreter really wants to be a manager of "the intercultural event of interpreting" (Roy 1993, 341), maybe she is the one who should resolve this problem because it is caused by obvious cultural differences. Roy (1989, 1993) and Metzger (1999) have already established and this chapter has corroborated that interpreters are no neutral, passive conduits and that they exert influence on the interaction, especially on the turn-taking process. Still, many interpreters try to maintain a position that is as neutral as possible and are very reluctant to consciously interrupt the interaction to make sure that all the Deaf participants are watching the signed interpretation. However, when the interpreter does not intervene, Deaf people end up not participating at mixed meetings.

SUMMARY

The data from this study show that two major differences occur between turn-taking mechanisms in all-sign meetings and turn-taking mechanisms in spoken language, multiparty conversations. One difference is that, in spoken language conversations, one of the most important means of allocating the next turn to someone was by affiliating a name or other identifying term to a sequence-initiating action whereas this method was never used in the all-sign meetings. Second, embedded addressing without eye gaze, another means of allocating the next turn in spoken language conversations, was never done in the all-sign meeting. On the contrary, in the all-sign meeting, eye gaze proved to be an extremely important and powerful regulator by which the current speaker selected the next speaker. A person could self-select in all-sign meetings by waving a hand, indexing, lightly touching the current speaker on the arm, tapping the table, stretching out a 5 classifier handshape (with the palm away from the speaker and the fingers up, just above the table), or asking another participant to warn the current speaker that the person wants the next turn. However, whoever self-selected as next speaker got the floor only when the current speaker (and not the chairperson) looked at him or her rather than at any of the other participants. So self-selection in all-sign meetings was never pure self-selection because the current speaker still had the power to allocate the next turn by means of eye gaze.

The system of turn allocation in all-sign meetings is completely different from the system that was used in mixed meetings with one or two sign language interpreters. One major difference was caused by a far more restricted use of gaze direction in mixed meetings. Deaf participants in mixed meetings had no control over the organization of turn-taking and the allocation of the next turn because their gaze direction necessarily was restricted to the interpreter. For the hearing participants, however, the situation was not all that different from chaired spoken language meetings because the chairperson was in charge and organized the allocations of the next turn.

Another difference was that the participants in mixed meetings had to signal to the chairperson that they wanted the floor. Consequently, Deaf participants had to break eye contact with the sign language interpreter and seek eye contact with the chairperson to signal for a next turn. This signaling to the chairperson was sometimes quite difficult, especially when the chairperson did not notice it. When something similar happened with the hearing participants (i.e., that the chairperson had not seen their signaling to ask for the floor), they simply supported their signaling by using their voices, and the chairperson immediately reacted to the sound. The Deaf participants, thus, depended on the interpreters when the chairperson had missed their signaling.

This whole process of signaling was even more difficult when only one interpreter was present. Often, one of the Deaf participants wanted to say something, but the chairperson hadn't seen his or her signal, and the interpreter couldn't warn the chairperson because she was still interpreting (either from sign to voice or from voice to sign). When the chairperson forgot about his or her role as coordinator of the meeting and forgot to allocate the next turn, the flow of participation was disrupted. Either people started talking at the same time and the interpreter was at a loss or (and this situation occurred especially when only one interpreter was present) people were speaking and signing at the same time, and the signing was not interpreted.

In the mixed meetings, self-selection of the next speaker happened infrequently and, then, only when the previous speaker was using the same language. So at those times, the turn nearly always went from Deaf person to Deaf person or from hearing person to hearing person, but never from hearing person to Deaf person or vice versa. Self-selection by a signer occurred only when the eye gaze of the previous signer was directed at him or her and not at the interpreter.

These instances were very similar to the ones found in the all-sign meeting. In all these cases, the gazes of the signers were directed at each other and not at the chairperson or at the interpreters. When a hearing participant self-selected, the interpreter had to indicate the transition. In the meeting with two interpreters, the voice-to-sign interpreter usually indicated this transition, but she sometimes forgot to do it, so in those cases, the Deaf participants were not aware of a change of turn.

Self-selection by a signer when a hearing person was speaking proved extremely difficult. In the meeting with only one interpreter, these attempts resulted in overlap and loss; thus, what the Deaf participants had signed was not interpreted into Dutch. In the meeting with two interpreters, self-selection by a signer proved difficult because of the "interpretational lag." During this lag, the interpreter has trouble determining the point at which he or she can interrupt the speaker to signal that the signer has self-selected (the signer also lags behind because he or she has to wait for the voice-to-sign interpretation). In the meeting with two interpreters, the problems caused by overlap were sometimes resolved by one of the interpreters, but sometimes the interpreters chose not to take the initiative and let the chairperson and the Deaf participants resolve the problems.

Roy (1993) claimed that interpreters have four options in the case of overlap, but the data discussed in this article suggest that, at least in multiparty conversations, a fifth option is available: The interpreter can choose to warn the interlocutors that overlapping talk is occurring and can let them resolve the conflict.

Finally the study identified a serious difference between the all-sign meeting and the mixed meetings with respect to making sure that everybody participates. In the all-sign meeting, a signer usually checked whether the other participants were looking at him or her. When the signer saw that a person was not looking, because he or she was reading something for instance, the signer would either tap the table or ask the neighbor to warn the person that conversation had started again. In the mixed meetings, this practice hardly ever occurred. In fact, quite frequently, a hearing person started talking and the interpreter started interpreting, but one or more Deaf people were not looking at the interpreter and nobody got their attention.

A similar phenomenon could be seen when papers were distributed during a meeting. When papers were distributed in the all-sign meeting, time was given for people to look at them. Afterwards, the person distributing the papers explained what was written down, showed the relevant passage to the whole group so everybody knew the passage about which he or she was talking, and then discussed it. When papers were distributed in the mixed meetings, no time was given to look at them. The hearing participants listened to the explanations and looked at the papers at the same time whereas Deaf participants needed to first read the papers and then look at the explanations, but were unable to follow this process without missing important information. Moreover, relevant passages were not shown to the Deaf participants. An alternative proposed in this study is that perhaps the interpreters could resolve this problem instead of attempting to act as a neutral, passive conduit, an attempt that is not possible to do anyway. This proposal strengthens Metzger's remark:

> Thus, the question for the field of interpreting becomes clear: should interpreters pursue full participation rights within interpreted encounters? Or should interpreters attempt to minimize, where possible, their influence within interpreted interaction? Herein lies the paradox of neutrality. (Metzger 1999, 204)

CONCLUSION

A common assumption is that the presence of a sign language interpreter creates equality between hearing and Deaf participants in a mixed meeting. However, this analysis clearly showed that, to obtain equality, at least two conditions need to be fulfilled. First, the chairperson needs to control the meeting tightly in the following ways:(a) allowing only one person at a time to talk or sign, (b) allowing ample time for the interpreters to interpret everything before reactions are invited, (c) glancing at all the participants (hearing and Deaf) on a regular basis to monitor which participants want to ask for the floor, and (d) ensuring that Deaf participants are looking at the interpreter as the conversation is progressing and, if papers are distributed, that sufficient time is given to Deaf people to first read the papers before talking about them. If the chairperson does not follow this practice (e.g., because he or she is not well acquainted with Deaf culture), then the interpreter's task should be to step out of his or her neutral role and resolve the problem, becoming a manager of "the intercultural event of interpreting" (Roy 1993, 341).

The second condition is that, in mixed meetings, at least two interpreters need to be present, one to interpret into the sign language being used and one to interpret into the spoken language being used, to guarantee optimal access to the conversation and minimal overlap. With only one interpreter present, overlap occurred more often and usually led to loss. With two interpreters (one sign-to-voice and one voice-to-sign), overlap could be resolved by one of the interpreters or by the chairperson who could then allocate the next turn to one of the participants. If only one interpreter is present or if the chairperson has no experience with Deafness and the interpreter assumes a neutral role, then the presence of a sign language interpreter will create only an illusion of equality. In this case, equal participation of both parties is out of the question.

REFERENCES

Baker, C. 1977. Regulators and turn-taking in American Sign Language. In *On the other hand: New perspectives on American Sign Language,* ed. L. Friedman, 215–36. New York: Academic Press.

Cokely, D. 1992. *Interpretation: A sociolinguistic model.* Burtonsville, Md.: Linstok Press.

Ehlich, K. 1993. HIAT: A transcription system for discourse data. In *Talking data: Transcription and coding in discourse research,* edited by J. Edwards and M. Lampert, 123–48. Hillsdale, N.J.: Lawrence Erlbaum Associates.

Larrue, J., and A. Trognon. 1993. Organization of turn-taking and mechanisms for turn-taking repair in a chaired meeting. *Journal of Pragmatics* 19(2):177–96.

Lerner, G. H. 1993. Collectivities in action: Establishing the relevance of conjoined participation in conversation. *Text* 13(2):213–45.

Metzger, M. 1999. *Sign language interpreting: Deconstructing the myth of neutrality.* Washington D.C.: Gallaudet University Press.

Roy, C. 1989. A sociolinguistic analysis of the interpreter's role in the turn exchanges of an interpreted event. Ph.D. dissertation, Georgetown University, Washington, D.C.

———.1993. A sociolinguistic analysis of the interpreter's role in simultaneous talk in interpreted interaction. *Multilingua* 12(4):341–63.

Sacks, H., E. A. Schegloff, and G. Jefferson. 1974. A simplest systematics for the organization of turn-taking for conversation. *Language* 50(4):696–735.

Wiener, M., and S. Devoe. 1974. *Regulators, channels, and communication disruption.* Research proposal, Clark University, Worcester, Mass.

Part 4 Language Attitudes

Deaf People in Bilingual Speaking Communities: The Case of Deaf People in Barcelona

Esperanza Morales-López, Delfina Aliaga-Emetrio, Jesús Amador Alonso-Rodríguez, Rosa María Boldú-Menasanch, Júlia Garrusta-Ribes, and Victòria Gras-Ferrer

Since the 1960s, the concerns of people who are deaf have evolved from being focused on exclusively pathological issues and now have acquired the dimensions that characterize any linguistic community. This transformation has occurred despite certain specific characteristics of deaf communities, among these, permanent contact with oral speakers. This fact has brought many researchers, mostly on the North American front, (e.g., see the other volumes in the series *The Sociolinguistics in Deaf Communities*, of which this book is a part) to study the consequences that the long-term situation implies from a sociolinguistic point of view: sign language that is used as a natural language by the deaf community and the corresponding oral language that is also a point of reference.

In addition, communities or groups of deaf people who are immersed in bilingual and multilingual oral communities are becoming more and more evident. This situation has led researchers to start paying more attention to these communities because of the important implications for the deaf child's education and for his or her family.

The sociolinguistic situation that is the object of our study is the bilingual situation of deaf people in the city of Barcelona where the spoken languages of both Catalan and Spanish are quite widespread among the population and also are used in the educational sphere. The situation in Barcelona is not as typical as in other Spanish regions where both Spanish and a native or first language is also spoken (Galicia, the Basque Country, Valencia, and the Balearic Islands) because, in these other areas, large segments of the population use only Spanish for daily communica-

We specially thank the presidents of Casal and Cerecusor who have opened the doors of their associations to us and all the deaf people who have contributed to our research. We hope to have properly interpreted their answers, we accept sole responsibility for these interpretations.

tion, and the educational system does not offer a widespread system of total immersion in both languages. For this reason, the Catalan situation is distinctive in linguistic terms, a case that leads us to suppose that, in Barcelona, trilingualism in deaf children may already be a fact.

In particular, our interest in this study is to analyze how the social and educational changes that have occurred in deaf communities all over the world in the last few decades have influenced the members of these deaf communities. That is, we address the following question: To what extent has the worldwide sociopolitical movement that claims a place for sign language in its own right (a process that we can say is well on the way to turning this mode of communication into a symbolic capital, in the sense that Bourdieu, 1992, has stated) affected the attitudes and uses of its users?

Inversely, we also set out to examine whether the educational changes in Catalan schools, which have established Catalan as the first medium of instruction, had had a similar influence on the deaf community. For this purpose, our research was focused on the opinions of a group of deaf people from two associations in Barcelona, which were gathered in response to a questionnaire designed for this purpose.

The majority of work published on multilingualism in deaf communities predominantly focuses on the situation in North America. In the United States, some studies have focused on Hispanic families who use Spanish at home and sometimes have little knowledge of English (many of whom are recent immigrants), but whose children go to school where the medium of instruction is both English and sign language (or any other variety of a mixture of oral language and signs). These studies (e.g., Delgado 1984; Gerner de García 1995; Christensen and Delgado 2000) deal with the case of deaf Hispanic children in the American educational system from different perspectives: (a) the studies highlight evidence that this group has a lower educational level than deaf White students (Lerman 1984; Delgado 2000; Ramsey 2000); (b) they observe the break that may—and, in fact, very often does—exist between the linguistic situation at home and at school (Carlise Dean 1984 and Fischgrund 1984 in Delgado 1984); and finally, (c) they confirm the fact that many of these families are immigrants with a low sociocultural level or, at least, with different sociocultural expectations (Gerner de García 1995; Ramsey 2000), a fact that further complicates the situation of trilingualism with which deaf children are faced. Finally, research by Cheng (2000) shows that deaf children from different Asian communities who are living in the United States present a similar case.

Other research on deaf communities in bilingual oral situations outside of North America has been carried out by Burns (1998) in Ireland, among others. Burns (1998) shows that the movement in favor of vindicating Irish Sign Language (ISL) has been enormously influenced by the movement to reclaim a position for the Irish language and by the efforts of American groups to defend ASL. However, this supposed trilingualism (ISL, Irish, and English) in the Irish deaf community is not yet an established fact because very few in this community actually have a real knowledge of the minority oral language—Irish (Burns 1998, 241). The same situation occurs in several Latin American areas where indigenous languages are still spoken. Hence, in the research by Johnson (1991) in a small Yucatec Mayan village, we observe that a trilingual situation (sign language, Maya, and Spanish) does not actually occur because deaf people do not have direct exposure to the native Maya language that is spoken by the majority of hearing people, in part, because most of the hearing villagers can sign. In addition, in similar autochthonous populations, Spanish is known by only a very limited part of the population, among them, children and young people who have attended school. Moreover, as Johnson points out, education is not generalized in this culture and even less so among deaf people in this culture. Finally, Jepson (1991, 39), in his research in India, briefly mentions the fact that deaf people also face a multilingual situation given the mosaic of oral languages that coexist in the country, although he does not discuss this aspect further.

CATALAN DEAF PEOPLE IN BARCELONA

Barcelona lies on the northeastern coast of Spain, and it is the capital of Catalonia, one of the three so-called historical communities in Spain with its own language (i.e., the Catalan language) in addition to Spanish. Catalonia's population is estimated to be 6 million, of which approximately 6,000 are members of the deaf community. The sociopolitical situation in Catalonia has witnessed important changes since the approval of the Spanish Constitution in 1978, which has turned the country into a parliamentary monarchy with a democratic government. In the Constitution, written by representatives from every political force in Spain, linguistic plurality was recognized for the first time. In addition to Spanish, which is official nationwide, Catalan is also granted official status within its own territory: "Castilian is the official language of the State . . . the other Spanish languages will also be official in their own Autonomous Community . . . the enrichment of the different linguistic modes in Spain is part of our cultural heritage and these are to be object of special respect and protection" (The Spanish Constitution, Preliminary Section, art. 3).[1]

Article 3 of the 1979 Statute of Autonomy of Catalonia states that "Catalan is the language of Catalonia . . . the Generalitat (the Autonomous Government of Catalonia) shall guarantee the official and normal use of both languages [Spanish and Catalan], as well as implement the necessary measures to ensure a knowledge of the languages and create the conditions that will allow equality in terms of the rights and obligations of the citizens of Catalonia."

The first law on linguistic normalization in Catalonia was promulgated in 1983. In the following years, different entities were created with the goal of spreading and recovering the use of Catalan. This period was the beginning of a time in which Catalan was institutionalized and, as Boix and Vila (1998) explain, new perspectives of study opened; language conflict, a key issue during the anti-Franco period, gave way to other priorities. Only one aspect of this model prevails through the mid-1990s, namely, *normalization* (this term has been widely used and accepted in Spain since it was first proposed by Aracil (1966) in the late 1960s to refer to government intervention directed at recovering the functions that a language either lacks or has lost).

Boix and Vila (1998) state that, during the first phase, from 1980 to the late '80s, the goal was to promote knowledge of the language and to foster a positive attitude toward the language; a second phase was to begin in the '90s, which was to promote its use and linguistic transmission in mixed (bilingual or multilingual) families, taking into account the effect of migrations. After long discussion on modifications in the law, a second law on linguistic normalization was approved in 1998.

Today, a quick glimpse at the process that has taken place over these last two decades of language planning in Catalonia gives us a clear indication as to how the Catalan language is stepping forward. The last lin-

---

1. Castilian is another name for Spanish; the term *Castilian* is preferred in the regions of Spain where another vernacular language exists because these other languages may also be considered "Spanish." In Latin America, however, many people prefer to use the term *Spanish* because it was the Kingdom of Castille (just before Spain's unification) that ordered their conquest. In this paper, we will use *Castilian* and *Spanish* as synonyms.

guistic census from 1996 shows that, in terms of any of the four language skills (listening, reading, writing, and speaking), the knowledge of Catalan is higher than ever before: In 1991, 74.3 percent declared they understood the language and 54.5 percent declared they could speak it whereas, in 1996, 95 percent declared they could understand the language and 75 percent declared they could speak it (see Direcció General de Política Lingüística 1996). One of the principal hallmarks of this language policy is that the educational system makes Catalan compulsory; every child is first exposed to oral and written Catalan, and Spanish is introduced only at eight years of age (for an update on the Catalan situation, see Pradilla 2001; Pujolar 2001).

Traditionally, from the linguistic point of view, deaf people in Barcelona and, generally, throughout Catalonia have been educated in Spanish. Although many of them are born to Catalan speaking families, in general, they have not been exposed to spoken Catalan, and consequently, they neither speak nor read this language. Oralism in Catalonia had always been in Spanish during Franco's time because Catalan was prohibited in formal settings. Although Catalan was spoken informally, hearing families with deaf members used Spanish when speaking to them.

The ban on Catalan may not have been so harsh outside the capital, Barcelona. A startling case is that of a woman now in her fifties, a member of Cerecusor association who was born in Sant Sadurní d'Anoia (a small village not too far from Barcelona) and who was not allowed to have any contact with the only other deaf boy in the village.[2] She learned Catalan as her first language, apparently, also at school because she can write Catalan. So her first exposure to Spanish was not until she was twenty and went to the capital, Barcelona, to study. There she met other deaf people for the first time and learned not only sign language but also Spanish. She married a deaf man from a deaf family in Barcelona who was skilled in written and oral Spanish. Today, she can speechread both languages, and she still speaks Catalan to hearing people. At home, her three hearing children are fluent in sign language, although they provide mouthed or verbal support in Catalan when talking to their mother while providing this support in Spanish to their father.

This situation is not a common one because the prevailing tendency among Catalan families in Barcelona still is to speak Spanish to deaf chil-

2. Cerecusor stands for Centro Recreativo Cultural de Sordos (Recreational-Cultural Center for the Deaf).

dren. Very often, educators have instructed their deaf students only in Spanish, and consequently, the deaf children will be able only to speechread this language. This situation is currently changing, and we will turn to this development when we analyze our data on the educational aspects of the interviews.

Deaf people have always used gestural signs to communicate in deaf families and also in the cultural associations of towns and cities all over Catalonia, as is done in the rest of Spain. In some cases, there were communities exclusively based on interactions and language use (similar to the cases described by Johnson [1991] and Branson, Miller, and Marsaja [1996]). In the last decade, influenced by other deaf communities in Europe, these groups have realized that the signed system they were using to communicate was, in fact, a proper language and, hence, have begun to work toward its social and political recognition. The effect that several conferences, symposia, and encounters have had on deaf identity, deaf culture, and signed language research has been so strong that we can definitely say that the 1990s have meant a huge step forward for the deaf community in Spain.[3] In relation to this development and following the tendency of the different European countries that have begun to claim their own signed languages as proper and minority languages, the Spanish deaf community has also expressed concern about the social and legal recognition of Spanish Sign Language (LSE).

Nevertheless, although this change is tangible among the leaders of the community or groups of deaf people, we know very little of the opinions of other members of the community, precisely those who are not involved directly with the political claims. We observe, however, that the attitudes of the general population and those of educational representatives in particular are also starting to change. This trend not only occurs to the detriment of oralism as an educational option but also affects intermediate solutions that involve a combination of oral and sign languages (communicative solutions that the Spanish deaf community refer to as *bimodal*). All in all, these trends are only intuitive because no research on attitudes similar to

---

3. Carol Padden's (1989) proposals on notions of community and culture as well as the work by Wilcox (1989) are very well known among Spanish deaf people. However, other later investigations such as Johnson and Erting's (1989) have had hardly any repercussion, although these authors offer a more dynamic definition of deaf communities in the sense that they consider interaction as the key to belonging to a deaf community.

the research on the American deaf community (e.g., Kannapell 1989, 1993; Ward Trotter 1989; Aramburo 1989) has yet been done. In addition, no research has been carried out similar to that of Lucas and Valli (1989, 1992) on the differences in structure and usage between sign language and bimodal forms.

Even though signing is not uniform, deaf people in general agree that they do, in fact, use the same sign language, namely, LSE. However, in Catalonia, because of greater differences between the signing of the Catalan deaf community and that of other communities in Spain, the Catalan deaf community increasingly feels that they use another sign language, which they term the Catalan Sign Language (LSC). A controversy has arisen between the two deaf groups because of this linguistic division.

Even though discussion on this matter is open and the Catalan parliament promulgated a bill for "promotion and spread of knowledge of LSC" in 1994, the Catalan Federation of the Deaf (Federació de Sords de Catalunya-FESOCA) has supported every measure that the National Confederation of the Deaf in Spain (Confederación Nacional de Sordos de España-CNSE) has taken to advance official recognition of LSE. And so, in 1997, when the CNSE collected up to 150,000 signatures from all the associations and federations of deaf people in Spain as a measure designed to put pressure on the Spanish government to study the case, the Catalan Federation actively participated in the process. As a consequence, a motion was passed in the Spanish parliament that required the Spanish government to detail the measures that should be adopted for the progressive recognition and implementation of sign language, and also called for the evaluation of this implementation and its consequences.

Later, in April 1999, another motion was approved by the Senate (in Madrid) that called for the Spanish government to intensify its work on behalf of the development of sign language as a basic language of the deaf community and commit to writing a report before the end of 1999, identifying their special educational needs along with the estimated budget proposals required for the various government administrations to carry out these programs. This report was submitted in October 1999. Needless to say, the results of this work on behalf of the deaf community that is taking place in the nation's capital, will have a direct effect on the Catalan situation. It also became evident that the autonomous government in Catalonia should play a part in applying certain social pressure to ensure the success of these programs, at least as far as the powers that have been transferred to the autonomous regions (such as education) will allow.

However, the autonomous government does not seem to be ready—at least, not until now—to make the motion of 1994 prosper.

Turning back to the language matter, for the moment, almost no linguistic research has been done to determine whether the differences between LSC and LSE lie in grammatical issues or whether they are merely a consequence of cultural-political factors.[4] For instance, cultural-political factors affect language in another region of Spain, Valencia (to the south of Catalonia), where a variation of Catalan called Valencian is spoken. The grammar is very similar to Catalan, and the two groups can understand each other. However, the people of Valencia seem to have a very strong feeling of being separate from Catalonia and of having their own language.

The only research on the issue of signing differences has been done by Stephen and Dianne Parkhurst (1998) on sign variation among different deaf associations in eighteen Spanish cities.[5] The study set investigating differences in lexical variation as its primary goal. A secondary and less clearly defined objective was to examine differences in mutual understanding and social attitudes. The results on lexical differences indicate that, from a total of 200 words, the lexical variation among eighteen Spanish cities (including Barcelona) ranged between 96 percent and 58 percent.[6] The general conclusions are the following:

1. Almost every city of the eighteen that were analyzed has its own sign language dialect.

4. From the point of view of linguistic description, little work has been done on LSE and LSC. The first research was that of Rodríguez González (1992). A description, though somewhat incomplete, of the phonetic and grammatical features of LSE is provided in Martínez Sánchez et al. (2000); for a description of LSC, see Fourestier (2002). A research group from the National Confederation of Spanish Deaf (Confederación Nacional de Sordos Españoles, or CNSE) that is responsible for developing educational materials has reedited the dictionary by Pinedo Peydró (2000) and has also published a basic LSE dictionary in CD-ROM format.

5. Some of the ideas presented here are not included in the article cited because the authors have personally provided us with this information directly.

6. A 0 percent–40 percent average is considered to indicate a different language family; 40 percent–60 percent different languages, but belonging to the same family; and 60 percent–70 percent, probably a different language although it would be necessary to compare these results with samples of mutual understanding.

2. The cities of every autonomous region constitute a separate dialectal group.
3. The differences are too few to consider the dialects as separate languages, so it is necessary to see the results of the tests on intelligibility.
4. Compared to signed languages from Portugal, Italy, France, México, and the United States, Spanish varieties can be considered part of a separate family of languages.

When the results from Barcelona were compared with the other cities studied, the similarity of Barcelona's signs with that of A Coruña was found to be 69 percent (the videos shown in one of the questions of the interviews was videotaped in this city) and 58 percent when compared with Santiago de Compostela (both A Coruña and Santiago de Compostela are in the northwestern part of Spain). In comparison, 71 percent of Barcelona's signs were similar to that of Madrid and 70 percent when compared with Zaragoza (near Catalonia). Finally, similarity with the signs of Valencia (south of Catalonia and a Catalan speaking community, as previously explained) was 69 percent. Although Valencia's signs had fewer differences than Catalonia's when each was compared to other communities, more differences were observed between Valencia's and Catalonia's signs than, for instance, between the signs of Valencia and those of Zaragoza (both near Barcelona).

The tests of intelligibility revealed that isolation was less than 75 percent for every dialect.[7] That is, in terms of mutual understanding, Stephen and Dianne Parkhurst (1998, 35) propose that any variety can be considered a separate language from the rest. However, in some cities (they do not specify which ones), the levels of intelligibility dropped to marginal levels. In terms of social attitudes (36), their study found that, despite the differences mentioned, informants all over Spain (except for Catalonia) asserted that they used the same language, LSE. In Catalonia, informants openly said that they signed LSC. At the same time, deaf people living outside Catalonia said that the deaf people of Catalan sign differently and that, sometimes, that group is difficult to understand.

7. The tests passed were based on Grimes (1995), where values between 100 percent and 85 percent were considered to show "appropriate understanding," values between 85 percent and 75 percent can be considered to border the limits of understanding; and values of less than 75 percent indicate that communication is not adequate.

With these conclusions as a starting point, we began our research focusing on two associations of deaf people in Barcelona, the most dynamic city of the region because of its status as the region's capital and as headquarters of the Catalan Federation of the Deaf. We expected to find some traces of most of the possible changes that have occurred within that deaf community in the last few years. The associations chosen were Casal de Sords de Barcelona (Home for the Deaf of Barcelona), or Casal, and Centro Recreativo Cultural de Sordos de Barcelona (Cultural and Recreational Center for the Deaf of Barcelona), or Cerecusor, each of which has a long-standing cultural and social tradition.

Casal de Sords de Barcelona is the modern name for an older association that was founded in 1916 by a group of deaf people who used to meet regularly in a café on Mallorca Street.[8] These groups of deaf people who met informally decided to create an association that would represent their interests and organize cultural and entertainment activities. To attract more members, they announced that every person who stated his or her interest in joining the project during 1915 would also be considered a founding member of the association. The association was formally founded in 1916 with twenty-eight members and was called Centro familiar de Sordomudos (The Family Centre for Deaf-Mutes). The statutes were not approved until 1919, and in 1924, the name of the entity was changed to Círculo Recreativo de Sordomudos (Recreational Centre for Deaf-Mutes). Two peñas (clubs) were created in 1927: One dedicated to sports activities and the other to organizing excursions for the young. After a period of separation in which each of these peñas created its own association, they joined together again in 1937 to form Casal de Sord-muts de Catalunya (Home for the Deaf-Mutes of Catalonia). Interestingly, this time, the name was in Catalan. This switch to Catalan occurred during the period known as the Second Republic, a period characterized by a general respect for minority languages. In 1940, after the Civil War (1936–1939), because of government pressure, the name had to be changed into Castilian again: Hogar del Sordomudo de Barcelona (Home for the Deaf-Mutes of Barcelona). For political reasons during Franco's regime, the association

8. The traditional word in Spanish for this kind of gathering is *tertulia*. They were very popular in the nineteenth century and part of the twentieth century when many intellectuals and artists would meet this way. Many cultural and intellectual events can trace their beginnings to these informal gatherings. From Spain, this tradition was passed on to cultural circles in Latin American countries.

was seriously endangered, managing to survive thanks to a politician of high rank whose son was a member of the association. In 1943, the association was renamed once more—Casa del Sordomudo de Barcelona (House for the Deaf-Mutes of Barcelona).

In 1949, the association hosted the First National Congress of Deaf-Mutes, and in 1956, an evening school was opened to provide literacy instruction for deaf adults. In 1975, the organization was finally able to have its own sites. One location was used as a meeting place and the other as a technical school. In 1985, the association moved to its present location on Tamarit street, in a working-class district, and in 1990, a new name was adopted: Casal de Sords de Barcelona (Home for the Deaf of Barcelona). The word *mute* was finally omitted from the name.

Today, the Casal association has approximately 500 members, thirty of whom are hearing, including eight who are hearing children of deaf parents. These hearing members are given the status of ordinary members; however, they have only the right to speak, not to vote, and no hearing person can be a member of the board.

According to what our informants report, the number of young members in the association has diminished since the practice of mainstreaming was begun in the educational system. However, we cannot precisely say that young deaf people who are not association members are not members of the deaf community, because they very often meet in front of the association, and they maintain a certain relationship with the older members, even though they are not full association members themselves.

The main activities that Casal organizes are conferences on different topics once a month, courses for lexical improvement, sign language courses for children, trips for adults such as visiting museums and excursions, day trips for the young, a biennial theater show, and soccer championships for all ages. Despite this activity, the general sense is that, in the past, members were more involved in the organization and participation was greater. Members think that, today, there is no relationship between socioeconomic status and membership in the association.

Cerecusor also has a long tradition, although the association was established more recently. It was founded in 1941 on the initiative of a group of deaf people who were associated with the Catholic Church, in particular, the lay movement called Acción Católica (Catholic Action), which was very active in Spain at that time. In its first stages, this association was closely linked to a similar association in Madrid, Acción Católica Nacional de Sordomudos (National Catholic Action for Deaf-Mutes), which had been created one year before. A member of the association in Madrid contacted a deaf man from Barcelona who had gone to Madrid on a business trip, and the idea flourished because a group in Madrid felt it was their duty to spread the Lord's word to the deaf community. That same year, the Catalan delegation was established in Barcelona with forty members. They temporarily set up in a room at the Instituto Educativo de Sordomudos y de Ciegos—*La Purísima* (Educational Institute for the Deaf-Mute and the Blind—La Purisima). This school has been closely linked to the deaf association from the very beginning. A few months later, the association settled in Gracia, an upper-middle-class district in Barcelona where the association has since remained.

In 1975, the name was changed to Asociación Católica de Sordomudos (Catholic Association for the Deaf-Mutes), which had to be changed again in the late '70s because of a misunderstanding with respect to the legal reforms for associations, which forced them to change the statutes and, consequently, the name of the association. The new name, which is the same today, became Centro Recreativo Cultural de Sordos de Barcelona (Cultural and Recreational Center for the Deaf of Barcelona), or Cerecusor.

Today, Cerecusor has approximately 400 members, ten of whom are hearing, including eight who have deaf parents. As at Casal, the hearing members are given the status of ordinary members; however, they have only the right to speak, not to vote, and no hearing person can be a member of the board.

Apparently, the number of young members fell five years ago, but at the present, young people's memberships are increasing again. The main activities organized by this association are theater (the *theatre biennal*), cinema (the *cinema biennal*), a symposium once a year on different topics, and the Pedro Segimón Awards (named after the first president of the association).

Members also agree that people generally used to be more active, and they point out that, in the past, they received more government grants to cover the expenses. The current general opinion is that people's reasons for becoming members have more to do with the cultural activities that are offered than with economic considerations or identification with a particular socioeconomic class.

The two associations have experienced a change in their social profiles in the last few years. Traditionally, deaf associations were frequented by deaf people and their families. Hearing children of deaf parents were the only hearing people to be seen in these contexts. However, because of the proliferation of courses on sign language for hearing people who are interested in learning the language and because of the professionalization of the role of the sign language interpreter, more and more nonrelated hearing members are joining the associations, although they are very often not proper members of the association.

METHODOLOGY AND ANALYSIS OF THE DATA

In our study, we chose to interview two groups of people with similar characteristics who were members of the two associations described above. The groups consisted of informants of different ages who were not actively involved in the language recognition movement. In the end, we selected sixteen people from Casal and eighteen from Cerecusor.

These informants were given the questionnaire in written form (see appendix A), but in cases where the informant had difficulty understanding the questions and writing the answers, the interviewer signed all the questions and translated the answers into written language. Most of the interviews were conducted by the two interpreters from our group, one at Casal and the other at Cerecusor, because they each had a personal relationship with one of the associations. Some of the interviews were carried out by deaf members of our team of researchers.

To complete the interview information, we videotaped two pairs of young informants engaged in a spontaneous conversation. They were asked to talk about the same topics: school, jobs, friendship, and general questions about signing. We wanted to know their opinions on these issues and, at the same time, use this spontaneous data to observe the structural differences between their way of signing and the signing observed in fragments of conversations shown in a videotape that was recorded in an association outside Catalonia (from the city of A Coruña in northwest Spain). This videotape comparison corresponds to the last question of the written interview (see appendix A).

Different methodologies of field research have been used in sociolinguistic research on linguistic attitudes, including direct and indirect methods. Among direct methods, we find methods that request informants to answer a written questionnaire or respond to certain questions in an interview. Indirect methods include various methods designed to find out the opinions of the selected subjects while keeping them unaware of the researcher's true intentions (e.g., the well-known method of using "masks" as in Lambert and Tucker (1972) and Ward Trotter 1989; see a summary of this method in Fasold 1987; Grosjean 1982; Kannapell 1993).

As mentioned above, the methodology used was primarily a questionnaire, a direct means of data collection. Nevertheless, some of the questions that were included were also intended to obtain indirect information. For this reason, our questions never stated categories such us *sign language, LSC, or LSE* but, instead, were expressed using generic substitutes such as *signs*. This approach allowed informants to use terms that were more clearly generated by them, which allowed us to find the greatest differences among our informants. Identifying these differences was, in fact, one of the major objectives of our research. All in all, as can be seen from the questionnaire (see appendix A), our questions never imply valuing responses based on some specific scale as in Kannapell (1993). Our choice does not mean that we think this valuing approach would be inappropriate, but our research was designed to be exploratory in nature, with an objective to pursue this issue further if the results prove to be satisfactory. Because of the results obtained in this study, we can now consider carrying out further research into linguistic attitudes.

Sociolinguistic research has also maintained different traditions with respect to the analysis of the empirical data. One of these traditions is based on the macroanalysis of data [using statistical analysis, as in Labov (1972) while the other is based on microanalysis and relies on interactional data as the source of the research, as carried out in interactional sociolinguistics and ethnography of communication (e.g., Gumperz 1982a, 1982b; Duranti 1994]. We have opted for this second methodology, although we introduce one important variation: We provide our informants with a written interview.

The reason for this variation is purely practical. As mentioned previously, this study was a first step, and we have opted for the simplest way to begin. In future research, we believe that videotaping interviews will be the best source of gathering data because the videotaped data can be used dually to observe both opinions about language and language variation. Thus, in certain cases, some contradictions between opinions and actual practices may be observed, as in the case of some of our informants who occasionally contradicted themselves in terms of what they said they signed and what they actually signed. Likewise, we are interested not only in the opinions themselves but also in the way they are reproduced and constructed in the interactive process (Gumperz 1982a).

Next, we will proceed with the analysis of the different responses to the interviews, which were categorized in blocks, or sections. In our discussion, we will follow the order of the questions in the interview, addressing each of the sections in turn (see appendix A).

Block 1: Personal Aspects

A total of thirty-four interviews were conducted. The gender and age distribution of our informants is shown in table 1. Of all the informants interviewed, only six were born in provinces outside Catalonia. One thing that stands out in terms of marital status is that only one female informant of all the married interviewees is married to a hearing man. We hardly ever see couples in which the deaf partner is the woman; we are more likely to find couples in which the deaf partner is the man. The woman in this case is thirty-six and became deaf at three months. She attended mainstreamed schools and is a member of Casal. The remaining twenty-three married informants all have deaf partners. This fact reinforces the notion that deaf people still rarely mix with hearing people in their intimate relationships (Johnson 1991). However, because the data we collected were exclusively based on deaf informants, a real contrast cannot be made on this point.

Nevertheless, the point is clearly relevant; given that approximately 90 percent of the deaf population is said to be born to hearing families, one could expect the rate of people who attend deaf associations to reflect this reality. Nevertheless, we see that half of the deaf people interviewed have deaf relatives, which leads us to conclude that the population we find in such a context is mainly what we call "traditional deaf," coming from families with genetic links to deafness (see table 2).

One can easily understand why the percentage of deaf association members who become deaf at an age when they have almost fully acquired oral language is very low. Most members of the deaf community acquire sign language either at an early age—if they have deaf relatives—or when

TABLE 1. *Ages and Gender of Informants*

Association	Female	Male	16–29 years	30–55 years	Over 55 years
Casal	11	5	3	10	3
Cerecusor	4	14	5	8	5

TABLE 2. *Deaf Relatives of Informants*

Relationship	Casal	Cerecusor	Total
Couples with children	10	11	21
Couples with at least one deaf child	1	6	7
Informants with no deaf relatives	9	7	16
Informants with deaf relatives	5	13	18
Informants with a deaf child as the only deaf relative	0	3	3

they first go to school and enter into contact with other deaf people. Many oral deaf youth now go to the association at age twenty or more, not having met another deaf person before and not having acquired knowledge of sign language, and they often form their own group because they feel different. Table 3 shows the age at which the informants acquired sign language.

The clear majority of the informants who have a job are manual workers: factory employees, cleaners, etc. The following excerpts are taken from the videotaped conversations with the informants during the part of the interview about working conditions for deaf people and the reasons why deaf people do not get good jobs:

- "Today, because written skills are in much demand to get a good job, deaf people cannot reach the level to get them."—a woman in her early thirties at Cerecusor
- "Employers only take us because they receive financial support and not because of our skills."—young man from Casal
- "We deaf should make the effort at school to get good qualifications; there is a high degree of absenteeism at school because deaf students cannot follow the class and so they get bored and give up soon."—the same woman from Cerecusor
- "With interpreters in the classroom you feel much comfortable."—the man from Casal

TABLE 3. *Age at Which the Informants Acquired Sign Language*

Age at Onset of Deafness	Casal	Cerecusor	Total
From birth to 1 year old	7	12	19
From 1 to 3 years old	7	5	12
Postlocutory age	2	1	3

Block 2: Educational Aspects

As explained in the previous section on Catalan, when the democratic system was restored in Spain, every sector of sociopolitical life in Spain experienced significant changes. With respect to education, the introduction of Catalan in the classroom meant a reorganization of the curriculum in general. This reorganization was done progressively, of course, as was the enactment of Ley de Integración del Minusválido (The Law for the Integration of the Handicapped), or LISMI, passed in 1982. The development of education for deaf people in this century shows clear differences before and after this law. Education for the deaf has changed completely in the sense that deaf students passed from the traditional schools for the deaf to mainstream schools, with changes in their syllabi and in the aid of support teachers. In Catalonia, a group of public technicians from Centre de Recursos Educatius per a Deficients Auditius (The Educational Resource Center for the Hearing Impaired), or CREDA, is responsible for this process. There is one CREDA in every area, and the one in Barcelona is called CREDA Pere Barnils, located in the old school Centro Municipal Fonoaudiológico, which many members of Casal attended when it was a school for the deaf. This team in Barcelona is made up of psychologists, speech therapists, audiometrists, and educators. First, the team diagnoses the child's special situation and recommends a suitable school, namely, mainstreaming or special education.

These professionals are also responsible for reforms and certain changes in the syllabus, releasing students from some subjects such as foreign language, music, sometimes sport, and very often, Catalan. As one of our video-recorded informants says, "While my schoolmates were taking English lessons or sport, I was getting some support teaching from the speech therapist, who knew a bit of signing and could make things be easily understood."

In many schools, although support teaching is not the speech therapist's duty, because of the scarce resources provided by the Department of Education, these professionals very often have had to take on other professional roles for these children such as that of support teacher or even interpreter. For many students, the few hours with the speech therapist were the only moment in a school day when they could learn something. As a consequence of mainstreaming, an amazing majority of deaf students were failures at school, and many of them left school before the secondary level. Since the last educational reform (known as Ley de Ordenación General del Sistema Educativo [LOGSE]), education is now compulsory until age sixteen, which has broadened educational expectations for all children, although it has made things more difficult for deaf students who have dropped out.

The problems that have arisen as a result of these reforms do not merely affect the educational system. As we can see from the data provided here, the school and the associations have been the two main cornerstones responsible for the socialization of deaf people. Most were born to hearing parents who could hardly provide them with any information about the world, and so the association became a major source of information, providing a set of peers and the opportunity to learn a language. However, the so-called integrated deaf student is very often the only deaf person in the school. Not being able to rely on their peers for information, these deaf students very often feel isolated. As Plann states in *A Silent Minority* (1997), "Oralism led to both the marginalization of Spanish Sign Language and the impoverishment of the curriculum."

Sign language has not been part of the curriculum, and no interpreters have been provided. However, this situation has begun to change in the last few years as some pilot bilingual programs in primary and secondary schools in Madrid and Barcelona have started education in both sign language and in oral language. Sign language interpreters have begun to be welcomed in the classroom as is the case of two public primary schools, Escola Tres Pins (Three Pine Trees School) and Escola Josep Pla (Josep Pla School). The former gives instruction for both hearing and deaf students, but deaf students have been grouped together. The latter provides instruction for deaf students and handicapped deaf students, but they tend to group together the students who are simply deaf.

The Consell de Cent Secondary school includes deaf students in regular classrooms, and beginning with the 2000–2001 academic year, two sign language interpreters have finally begun to interpret some subjects. Each of the four deaf students have eight hours of interpretation a week, so they are forced to choose which subject they need most to be interpreted. Finally, another secondary school, Centre d'Educació Especial de Reeducació Auditiva de Sabadell (CRAS), in Sabadell, a town near Barcelona, also employs two sign language interpreters for its deaf students (see more information on these educational centers in Bellés, Cedillo, González de Ibarra, and Molins 2000).

As discovered during the interviews, most of the deaf informants in their teen years lack a knowledge of Catalan as a consequence of the adaptations made in their curriculum as previously mentioned. However, the multilingual situation in Catalonia and the use of the bilingual method—sign language used with oral language—are forcing educators to take into account using the three languages—LSC, Catalan, and Spanish—together. Because Catalan has become a language of prestige and the language of instruction for all children, parents and educators want to teach both Catalan and Spanish to these children so they can achieve greater social integration. In this sense, many parents of deaf children now not only are against syllabus reform but also want their children to be able to read and write Catalan.

The two pilot bilingual schools expect to achieve this purpose and introduce Catalan as the first written language of instruction as in any ordinary hearing classroom in Catalonia. However, because these deaf students do not receive any input in Spanish at all, in contrast to hearing children who are exposed to it from simply hearing it on the street or on television, they may have no background knowledge of this language when writing in Spanish begins, usually at the age of eight. We must also consider the case of non-Catalan speaking families, the majority of which have emigrated from other parts of Spain, and new immigrant families from Latin America or Africa, who have settled in the area in the last few years and who are often at a disadvantage in terms of their sociocultural background. Given this context, the situation in the near future could parallel that of the Hispanic or Asian deaf people in the United States (Christensen and Delgado 2000). This situation may bring about a break, as has already occurred in some cases (Christensen and Delgado 2000), between the family and the school where instruction is mainly conducted in sign language and Catalan. In the same way, we have observed that all deaf adults speak and hence speechread only Spanish and so are not able to speechread their own children's production in Catalan or that of any other young members of the deaf community.

In the last few years and in cooperation with these bilingual projects, many hearing parents have started to learn sign language, and a very popular association of parents of deaf children in support of these programs was created in the mid 1990s called Associació de Pares de Nens Sords de Catalunya (APANSCE).

As we have seen, the trilingual situation of these deaf children and young people who are already present in some schools of Barcelona poses a true challenge for educators and applied linguistic researchers in terms of ensuring competence in the three languages (to this trilingualism we also need to add a foreign language).[9] As explained in Oviedo (1996), bilingualism is not a solution per se unless this program provides adequate professionals and educational resources. As an example, Oviedo refers to the situation in Venezuela, where although bilingualism is accepted by law, it has not been successfully carried out. However, the success of deaf education in Denmark (Hansen 2002), for instance, contrasts Oviedo's example.

When our informants were asked about their schools, in general, those over the age of thirty or thirty-five answered that they had gone to deaf schools; those under that age said that they had attended mainstream schools. We can see an important difference between the two associations in terms of the groups who attended deaf schools, as we explained in the background information on Catalan. Most of the deaf members of Cerecusor come from different La Purísima schools that existed in different parts of Spain. Although most of them have attended the center in Barcelona, some have also attended the same school in Granada, Madrid, or Zaragoza. Only one of the informants (seventy-nine years old) said that, before the civil war (1936–1939), he had gone to Escuela Municipal in Barcelona and, after that, he had gone on to La Purísima in Barcelona.

The group of deaf informants of this same age group (thirty to thirty-five) from Casal come from a diversity of schools for the Deaf: three in Barcelona—Escuela Municipal (City School); Centro Fonoaudiológico (Phono-Audiological Center), which substituted for Escuela Municipal; and Centro Médico de Audición y Lenguaje and Purísima (Medical Center for Hearing and Language, and La Purísima), which is only one center—and one in Madrid—Colegio de Sordomudos de Madrid (School for the Deaf-Mute in Madrid).

We should point out that La Purísima was a private and religious school, and Centro Médico only private, whereas the rest were public schools. Our informants answer that, except for Centro Médico (oral education), deaf students used signs in the rest of the schools as a means of communication with their peers, and some even learned to sign precisely at school. Sometimes, lay teachers or nuns also used signs in some subjects. Thus, we observe that, although the tendency at the time was the oral method of education, signs constituted for these deaf students a means of socialization within the school experience.

9. In the paper by Bellés et al. (2000) already mentioned, this trilingual situation is not considered. The authors take into account only the bilingual situation that includes sign language and Catalan.

The informant who went to Escuela Municipal before the war and to Purísima after the war explains that he used to sign more in the first school than in the second. This fact is relevant because Escuela Municipal, founded in the 1920s, set out to be a pioneering example of a secular public school that followed the Montessori method of teaching, an innovation that was very fashionable at the time. This development took place during the period of the Second Republic, exactly during the time our informant attended Escuela Municipal.

This example seems to indicate that this movement in favor of educational reform that began in the 1920s in Spain had an effect on the oral method of the time. It is also relevant that a religious school such as *La Purísima* allowed signing during some of the lessons and that some of the nuns even participated at a time of such conservatism, as Franco's regime (1939–1975) is characterized.

As explained in the introductory section, this difference in educational background can be traced all through the history of the two associations. Members of Cerecusor were mainly from *La Purísima* whereas members of Casal attended mainly public schools for the deaf. This difference (private versus public school education) is also one of the reasons behind the traditional social differences between the associations, which would explain the lack of contact between the two. This difference is confirmed by what two of our young informants say in the video recording:

- "Between the two associations there is no communication or contact; I don't understand."—a young deaf man in his twenties
- "It is not an easy subject. Before, each association was a way to continue the social bond beyond school, but now with mainstreaming everything is more spread apart."—a young woman older than the man

The group of informants between thirty-five (approximately) and seventeen say that they attended mainstream schools, most of them public, where sign language was used neither in the classroom nor with their peers. Some were the only deaf students at the school. In contrast, other informants have attended some of the primary and secondary schools that are developing the bilingual oral language and sign language pilot project described above.

Finally, in terms of the level of studies reached, most of the adults (forty years and older) answer that they have completed the basic level (primary school). A group in their thirties have completed secondary education, having received training in technical schools (what is called Formación Profesional), and the youngest have attended Enseñanza Secundaria Obligatoria (Compulsory Secondary Education, also known as *E.S.O.*) until age sixteen. None of them have gone on to university, which gives us some indication as to their current or past occupations (see appendix A, section 1).

Block 3: Communicative Aspects

This part of the questionnaire is the longest and is the one dealing with linguistic uses.

RESPONSES TO QUESTIONS

A) How do you communicate with deaf people? And with hearing people?

The first few questions relate to the usual means of communication between a deaf person and a hearing person. If communication is carried out in signs with a hearing person, what is the difference in the signs used with him or her and those used with a deaf person?

Often, all our informants communicate with hearing people in oral language, but this oral language is Spanish. Only two young informants state that they use either Spanish or Catalan (one out of the eighteen informants from Cerecusor and one out of the sixteen informants from Casal). Of the older informants, only one from Cerecusor (fifty-five years old, deaf since the age of one) states that she uses both oral languages. Informants use sign language with other deaf people as well as with other deaf relatives and the association. They also use sign language with hearing people who know signs. Some informants say that they do not notice any difference when they sign to hearing people; however, many of them say that they sign differently with a hearing person than with a deaf person. The following reasons for the difference are given by the informants in both Cerecusor and Casal:

- Communication is different because they lack expression; thus, communication with hearing people is not as clear as with deaf people.
- Communication is different depending on the hearing person's proficiency in sign language. It is different because the way a deaf person thinks is different from the way a hearing person thinks.

- Communication is easier or more difficult depending on the sign language teacher that the hearing person has had.
- Communication is different because the signs of a hearing person are of a higher level that those of a deaf person. The hearing have more information; some of the signs they use are not understood by deaf people.
- I feel embarrassed to use signs with a hearing person; I think he or she is not going to understand me.

The variety of responses to this question are relevant from a linguistic and sociolinguistic point of view. First, we find structural reasons for the signing differences: hearing people do not master the richness of sign language, and some of them are not able to communicate fluently or not able to comprehend the signs completely. Thus, the deaf person has to adapt his or her way of signing. Second, we find cognitive reasons: hearing people and deaf people think differently. Last, we find social reasons: communication varies depending on the sign language teacher a person may have had for sign language instruction; deaf people are not familiar with the signs the hearing people use; and deaf people sense that hearing people are able to sign better because they have information that deaf people do not have.

Finally, from responses to the question on how the informants communicate, we can highlight what term they use to refer to the form of their communication. Knowing about the current controversy over establishing LSC as a separate entity from LSE, we avoided mentioning these terms when we designed the interview. Instead, we always used the term *signs,* without mentioning the notion of language at any time (see appendix A). In some cases, our informants wrote the answers themselves, and in other cases, the interviewees translated what the informant was signing at that moment into written Spanish. Table 4 shows the names that informants from Casal and Cerecusor use for sign language. The table also shows the ages of the informants who used each term.

What these labels reveal can be interpreted in the following way: the youngest informants (teenagers, people in their twenties, and some in their thirties) and very few of the older informants (parents of an LSC teacher) use the terms *LSC* and *LSE*. The rest (including some informants in their thirties) use *hands, signs,* or *mime.* This difference is evident proof of the social changes that have occurred in the deaf community in Catalonia in the last decade. At some point, some people began to use the term

TABLE 4. *Names for Sign Language*

Association	Term Used	(Age of Informants)
Casal	Sign language	(19, 32, and 70)
	LSC	(35, 36, and 37)
	Signs	(35, 36, 48, and 53)
	Language in signs	(26)
	Hands	(16 and 83)
	Mime	(84)
	Other answers	(35 and 46)
Cerecusor	LSC	(17, 20, 82, and 85)*
	LSC and LSE	(17)**
	Signs	(33, 38, and 72)
	Hands	(31, 34, 40, 53, 69, and 70)
	Mime	(31)
	Other answers	(23, 28, and 55)

*We have to point out that these two last people, aged 82 and 85, are married and their daughter is a sign language teacher.

**This person explicitly mentioned that he uses LSC and that the rest of Spain uses LSE.

LSC to refer to their traditional gestural communication while others continued to use the traditional terms *hands, signs,* or *mime.*

As explained in the introductory section, it was only one decade ago that deaf people in Spain became aware of the deaf movement taking place around the world for the recognition of signed languages. Consequently, they began to use the term *language* to refer to their own signing, LSE, with the exception of Catalonia. In Catalonia, because of traditional linguistic differences, a group of deaf people began to claim that the variation used there was, in fact, a different language—LSC. This group includes those with higher levels of education: leaders who work for the federation, sign language teachers, and the youth studying in the new bilingual programs.

In our choice of informants, we have avoided these literate deaf and have interviewed only deaf informants who have no direct relationship to the language by way of their job or current schooling and who do not have any special responsibilities in the community. In general, our interviewees have been high school students (who are not in bilingual programs) and manual workers. The difference in their responses shows that this movement for the recognition of LSC as a separate language has not reached the whole deaf community. This finding leads us to conclude that, in the two associations studied, despite being located in the same general area in the center of Barcelona (a city that is generally very open to new ideas), the news of this shift has not yet reached everyone; the information has not filtered down to all members of the community. However, for the moment, because of the limitations of our data, we need to be cautious and cannot suggest that this conclusion is generalizable to all of Catalonia.

Among the names used for oral language, table 5 lists the terms that are explicitly stated by informants from Casal and Cerecusor (not all of them answered this part of the questionnaire).

Most interviewees still maintain the traditional names for oral language: *oral language, oral way* or *oral expression, speech,* and even *mouth* (as opposed to *hands*). Very few people use the terms Spanish or Castilian; two of the informants who do are the couple from Cerecusor whose daughter works as a sign language teacher. This fact suggests that they are perhaps among the most literate people in the group. These answers about the names used to refer to oral language also reveal, as with the terms used for signs, that the sociolinguistic changes that some members of the deaf community (mainly, those who have reached a higher level of education) have experienced have not yet had the same effect on this group.

B) Do you ever join courses or conferences in sign language? Do you watch signed TV or captioned?

All informants answer that they attend courses or lectures in the deaf association of which they are members. In this sense, the two informants

TABLE 5. *Names for Oral Language*

Association	Terms Used	(Age of Informants)
Casal	Oral language	(26)
	Oral expression	(46)
	Oral way (in Spanish, *oral*)	(16, 19, 32, 35, 35, 35, 36, 36, 37, 48, 53, 70, 83, 84)
Cerecusor	Language	(33)
	Oral way (in Spanish, *oral*)	(17, 17, 20, 30, 31, 34, 38, and 55)
	Mouth	(31)
	Speech (in Spanish, *habla*)	(23, 53, and 69)
	Castilian	(72, 82, and 85)
	Other answers	(31 and 70)

from Cerecusor who were videotaped say that the main difference observed between the two associations is that Cerecusor organizes more cultural events and Casal organizes more youth activities such as sports or outdoor events.

In reference to signed television programs, almost all of them say (either explicitly or implicitly) that, every Saturday morning at 10:30, they watch the program *En otras palabras* ("In Other Words"), which is produced in Madrid by the Spanish public television channel (TVE-2).[10] They also know of other signed programs, such as *Bon dia, Catalunya* ("Good Morning, Catalunya") that is on TV3 at 8:30 A.M., but they cannot watch them because the shows are broadcast in the morning and they are not at home at that time.

When asked about the differences between the signs used in these television programs, the majority of the informants referred to the program *En otras palabras.* In general, they notice differences that they explain with the reasons shown in table 6.

Table 6 shows that, once again, only some informants use the names LSE and LSC to refer to the differences between their way of signing and signing by other Spaniards. But on some level, all the informants recognize that these differences do, in fact, exist.

In general, informants watch captioned programs. However, we need to point out that not many of these programs are broadcast.

C) Do you know any Spanish deaf people outside Catalonia? Do you understand them when they sign?
With the exception of two people, all of the informants have had contact with other deaf Spaniards. All of the informants in both associations also claim a mutual understanding with deaf people all over Spain, although they notice that there are language differences. Table 7 lists some of the reasons given for these differences.

10. This half-hour program first aired two years ago, with signing partly in bimodal form and partly in LSE. One section of the program is a summary of the week's national and international news, and another focuses on news about the deaf community. Although the program has been criticized for using bimodal signing and because only one deaf person participates, the number of deaf viewers has increased, even in Latin America, as indicated by the letters of support the program has received.

TABLE 6. *Reasons for Differences in Signs Used on Television Programs*

Association	Terms Used	(Age of Informants)
Casal	They are different because of the form of the signs	(35, 46, and 83)
	They are a bit different	(53)
	They are different languages	(26, 35, and 37)
	Other answers	(19, 32, 35, 36, 36, and 36)
	No explanation about differences	(16, 36, 48, 70, and 84)
Cerecusor	They are signs from Madrid	(17, 28, 33, 53, and 69)
	They are their own signs (answer used the sign glossed as SUYO, or "theirs"	(38)
	They are different signs	(40)
	There are only a few differences	(34)
	There are differences because it is a different language ("the difference is LSE vs. LSC")	(17, 23, 55, and 72)
	The difference is little, but they are LSE and LSC	(82 and 85)
	No explanation about differences	(31, 31, and 70)

D) Do you know any foreign deaf people? Do you understand them when they sign?

One group of informants said they knew foreign deaf people because they have traveled abroad or because they have met foreigners who have come to Barcelona. Most informants agree that foreigners sign very differently. Some do not understand deaf foreigners and others understand them for the following reasons:

- The parties resort to the international sign system.
- The parties use mime, facial expression, or clearer signs.
- One informant (age seventeen) can speechread English, which helps in understanding the foreigners.

TABLE 7. *Reasons Given for Sign Language Differences between Catalonia and Other Parts of Spain*

Association	Terms Used	(Age of Informants)
Casal	They are different	(36 and 48)
	They are a bit different	(16, 35, 35, 37, 46, 53, and 83)
	They are very different	(19, 26, 32, 35, 36, 36, 70, and 84)
Cerecusor	There are differences, but small ones; or small	(17, 28, 31, 34, 55, 72, 82, and 85)
	differences because every city has its own signs	(33)
	They are different but we understand them because of mouthing; or	(20, 23, and 70)
	because of the contact over the years	(69)
	I understand, but the difference is the structure	(38)
	Barcelona is more different to Madrid than Zaragoza (a city closer to Barcelona, but not part of Catalonia)	(40)
	"Catalonia is the most different in all of Spain. Lérida (another Catalan city) is more similar to Madrid. But we understand each other"	(53)

E) Do you use interpretation services? Do you sign differently to interpreters? Do you understand them when they sign?

Almost half of the informants from Cerecusor do not use interpretation services for personal use. However, this average is lower for the group from Casal (four people do not use this service, but eleven people do). The majority of informants from both associations do not sign differently to interpreters. However, a small number notice some differences, except in cases where the interpreter was born to a deaf family. Table 8 shows the answers that were given with respect to understanding interpreters.

In general, we observe that interpretation services are not used by everyone, although those who do not use them represent an ever decreasing minority. The informants attributed no differences in actual commu-

TABLE 8. *Responses about Understanding Interpreters*

Response	Age of Casal Informants	Age of Cerecusor Informants
Do not have problems understanding	32, 35, 35, 36, 46, 53, and 83	16, 17, 17, 20, 23, 28, 33, 53, 55, 69, 72, and 85
Do have problems understanding	36	70, 82, and 84
Whether I understand depends on the person who is interpreting	19, 35, 37, 48, and 70	31, 33, and 34

nication to age; informants note that the differences observed are more often because of individual differences on the part of the various interpreters. One interesting comment among the opinions expressed by the two young men from Casal who were videotaped was that interpreters should be qualified professionals. Note that interpretation services in Catalonia are insufficient as a result of the minimal support from the regional government for those services. This tendency seems to have begun to change because, since this academic year (2000–2001), sign interpretation studies are now given at one high school in Barcelona.

F) Where do you the think people in the videotape are from?

Finally, the last question of our interview sets out to determine the extent of the differences identified in answers to previous questions. Informants were asked to identify the city or region where the people shown on videotape were from. Although there was some difference of opinion, the majority agreed that the informants came from an association from outside Catalonia. To remind our readers, the video was recorded in the city of A Coruña, in the northwest of Spain, and Barcelona is located in the northeast. Table 9 lists the answers given by the two associations.

As we can see, our informants have difficulties in recognizing the specific city or region. Nevertheless, almost all of them agree that it is an association outside Catalonia; however, three people say it is outside Barcelona, but still Catalonia. Only two people were able recognize the right place, A Coruña, but one of them actually knew people from there. This difficulty in recognizing regional differences in signed languages contrasts sharply with the ease of recognizing differences in oral Spanish and Catalan languages, which exhibit significant phonetic and lexical differences

TABLE 9. *Responses Identifying from Where the Two Videotaped Informants Came*

Response	Age of Casal Informants	Age of Cerecusor Informants
Outside Catalonia	19, 37, 46, and 83	31, 31, 33, 34, 55, 72, 82, and 85
From Madrid	16 and 70	
From Galicia and A Coruña	35	38
Outside Barcelona	36	
From the Basque Country	84	
From Catalonia		17 and 40
From Mataró (a big town in the province of Barcelona)		28
I do not know	48	
It is LSE	36	20, 23, 31, and 33

that are easily recognizable by speakers from the different regions. Deaf people explain this difference between oral and signed languages as stemming from the specific history of signed languages. Deaf people have learned signing at schools, and their distinct way of signing is, to a certain extent, more directly related to those schools. At the same time, one of the most important deaf schools in Spain has been La Purísima, run by a religious order that has several schools for the deaf in Spain. The nuns who teach in these schools are often sent by their congregation from one school to another. Some of the religious knew sign language, which could have served as a means of transmitting signs from one school to another. In addition, when a deaf student moved to another city, he or she would usually go to go to a branch of La Purísima (which is the case for some of our informants). Johnston (1998) gives an outstanding example of this kind of difference, which involves a hand alphabet in Australia. After arriving in Australia, two different deaf communities, the Anglican British and the Catholic Irish, adopted different systems: those who were Catholic adopted the one-handed alphabet whereas those who were Protestant adopted the two-handed, British alphabet.

When informants were asked whether they understood what was said in the videotape, most responded affirmatively. Only a few had problems understanding, and only one person (age thirty-six, from Casal) barely could understand anything.

After collecting the informants' answers, the next step was to analyze the particular differences that could be observed in the recording. The linguistic analysis of the recording was carried out by the researchers (three who are deaf, one who is hearing and bilingual, one who is a linguist and interpreter, and another who is a linguist). The main differences observed are related to lexical variation. However, this variation can be classified according to different levels, using only linguistic criteria:

1. The signs are different because there is no formal similarity in terms of the parameters.
2. The signs are different, but some or several of the formational parameters are similar: location, movement, or configuration.
3. The signs for the same concepts are different, but it is important to note that, all over Catalonia, other signs are also used to refer to the same item; some of them coincide (totally or partially) with the one used in A Coruña or in a city nearby.
4. There is similarity between the signs used in the video and in Barcelona.
5. The same sign has a different meaning in the two cities. This difference indicates a semantic change.

The following is a list of the signs that can be classified into the first category (no formal similarity in terms of the parameters):

Nouns—FROG, MISS, TOMORROW, SHOE, WEDNESDAY, MAY, and WEDDING
Adjectives—HAPPY, BROWN, and CURIOUS
Verbs—WARN, BEGIN, WAIT, and HAVE
Idioms and other grammatical forms—I CAN'T, I DON'T KNOW, WHY, and THERE IS OR THERE ARE

The second category (different signs, but some or several of the formational parameters are similar: location, movement or configuration) is represented by the following signs:

Verbs—DISAPPEAR, HEAR, TEST, SAVE, CONTEMPLATE (or ADMIRE), FRIGHTEN, TELEPHONE and FEEL-LIKE
Nouns—TREE, MOTIVE, WRONG, FEAR, LIE, BEDROOM and SMELL
Adjectives—EASY

In the third category, we include different signs that are used for the same concept, but we must point out that, all over Catalonia, other signs are also used to refer to the given item, and some of these other signs adopt the same form as the sign used in A Coruña. In this category, only three signs have been noted: PERRO (dog), NIÑO/HOMBRE (child or man), and CONOCER (know). One example of the opposite situation is the sign TO WORK. In Catalonia, only one sign for WORK is used, but this sign is similar to one of the signs used in Galicia to indicate *work*.

In the fourth category (similarity between the signs used in the video and in Barcelona), we include similar signs:

Nouns—CONTACT, ROOM, and BED
Adverbs—BEFORE
Verbs—LIVE, LICK, TAKE, FALL, FLY, WAKE UP, WALK, BELONG TO, SCREAM, and LOOK-FOR

The fifth category is reserved for signs that have the same form but a different meaning in the two cities: NOW (in A Coruña) and QUICK (in Barcelona); WHICH (in A Coruña) and HOW (in Barcelona).

The following five differences in morphology were observed. First, to express the meaning ONE-DAY, TWO-DAY (and so on), a distinct form and combination is used:

- In Barcelona, the sign DAY is formed with location on the upper part of the head, followed by the number, as in DAY-ONE, DAY-TWO.
- In A Coruña, the sign DAY is formed with only one hand, with no location on the head or body, and the number is incorporated.

This difference in how the numeral is expressed is not properly a morphological distinction but a phonological constraint arising from the different configuration of the two signs used. For this reason, it has to be considered as a lexical variation that manifests itself at the morphological level.

In the second difference, the numerical order in expressions like TWO-CHILDREN (or NEPHEW, etc.) is different:

- In Barcelona, the expression would be glossed as CHILDREN-TWO.
- In A Coruña, it is glossed as TWO-CHILDREN.

However, in Barcelona, the answer to the question How many children do you have? would also be TWO CHILDREN, with topicalization of the numeral. Fernández Soneira (2000) explains how this variation in numerical order is also evident in her empirical data from Vigo (a city close to A Coruña).

The third difference shows a different order in the expression "at night, very late":

- In A Coruña, it is signed VERY-LATE NIGHT
- In Barcelona the expression is signed NIGHT VERY-LATE.

The fourth difference involves the meaning of "work hard," which, in Barcelona, is expressed with the sign WORK and a facial expression to indicate the intensity of the work. In the videorecording of A Coruña, one can observe that two signs are used: TRABAJAR DOBLE (WORK-DOUBLE). We believe this form is borrowed from the popular Spanish expression *trabajar doble* because the form used in Barcelona is also used in A Coruña.

The fifth difference involves differences in the forms used to express numerals. However, great variation occurs all over Spain. For instance, the forms used in A Coruña are different from those used in Madrid, although in LSE courses for hearing students, both types of forms are taught.

Finally, the last step in our analysis was to observe possible linguistic differences between the two recordings of Casal and Cerecusor because, as explained in the introduction, these two associations have traditionally attracted people from different schools. Our analysis has discovered only minor variations on the lexical level:

- Use of the same signs (e.g., FEAR and TELEPHONE) but with some difference in parameters. The deaf researchers explain the difference in signs for TELEPHONE as arising from the distinct origin of this verb: Deaf people from La Purísima school make this sign with only the index finger as part of the hand configuration whereas deaf people from the municipal school use two fingers.
- Use of a distinct lexical form for the same expression. To express "The deaf are able to work like hearing people do," our Casal informants sign MANOS-CAPACES (literally, hands are capable) and our Cerecusor informants sign MANOS-BUENAS (hands are good).

However, some interference from LSE has been observed in the interaction recorded on videotape. According to the deaf researchers, the two informants from Casal use the morphological expression in which the numeral is incorporated in the sign MES (month), and they observed some interference from LSE in one of the informants from Cerecusor.[11] This

11. We have chosen not to specify this person's identity or sex.

informant has lived in different parts of Spain and uses signs from these areas. However, in the interaction, this informant, who was born deaf, makes linguistic judgments about the way the interaction partner (who, though deaf, has achieved oral literacy) signs.

INTERPRETATION OF THE DATA

At the beginning of our research, we set out to achieve two goals. First, we intended to analyze the changes that have occurred in the last decade within the deaf community as a whole by studying language recognition by two groups of informants from two associations in Barcelona. Second, we were also interested in examining whether and how the linguistic changes that have taken place in Catalonia in the last twenty years (after public recognition of the vernacular language) have had an effect on the deaf community.

From the analysis of the interviews, we have obtained meaningful data relevant to the first of our goals. With respect to the second goal, we have observed that the Catalan language has no relevant position among those in the deaf community. We suspect that this observation will need to be taken into account in the future when the bilingual programs that have recently been started (sign language with Catalan and Spanish) are completed. However, as we will explain below, the movement claiming a place for Catalan may have some effect on some decisions made by the deaf community.

At this point, we will focus on the first of our goals, the influence of foreign ideas on the opinions of our deaf informants. From the analysis of the data, several points need to be highlighted.

Concerning the set of questions on literacy aspects, once again, we observe the strong influence that deaf schools and traditional cultural associations have had as the main arena for socialization and sometimes as the only places where deaf children of hearing parents can learn sign language. This natural relation between schools and cultural associations (as shown in the case of Casal and Cerecusor) comes to an end in the 1980s when mainstreaming is imposed in the educational system in Spain and deaf students are integrated into ordinary schools with other hearing students.

Some of our youngest informants have already studied in those mainstream schools and, in those cases, their contact with the deaf world has been reduced to contact with cultural associations or family (if they were born into a deaf family). Our informants' opinions about this educational methodology coincide with the findings from other research (e.g., Ramsey 1997; Burns 1998): a general rejection of mainstreaming, which has not achieved one of its main goals—literacy for deaf people. Because of this educational failure, deaf leaders have been looking at foreign bilingual programs for deaf children with a view to carrying out similar programs as pilot projects in Spain.

In terms of communicative issues, several points should be highlighted. First, we can say that, in general, our informants seem to agree that signing has been their natural way of communicating with other deaf people and has been a tool for strengthening social relations. This consensus explains why they continue meeting in their cultural associations despite their lack of social recognition.

Another communicative issue is the change in the name for the traditional form of communication; a new term is used by some of the informants. Instead of the usual terms *signs, hands,* or *mimic,* this group used the term *language.* The same group (those who identify their particular way of signing as a language) compare the Catalan way of signing to signing in the rest of Spain (acknowledged by almost all of the informants as their characteristic form of signing) and make a clear distinction between their own variety and the one outside Catalonia, naming them LSC and LSE, respectively.

This distinction could be considered a spontaneous development because of linguistic differences. However, because this phenomenon is not widespread, an alternative reason could be that this distinction is a movement initiated and planned by a specific sector. Some of our informants express their disagreement with the way in which the introduction of neologisms are formally planned and implemented. In particular, one informant noted that sign language teachers invent new signs that other deaf people cannot understand; another explains that the degree to which he understands hearing signers depends on the sign language teacher who taught them. Therefore, a certain intervention in the language is observed: modifications that do not arise spontaneously and that are not shared by all of them. That is, changes in the language are made intentionally and separately from everyday use, and news of these changes has not reached all the members of the deaf community.

In analyzing this distinction further, two ideas stand out. First, the fact that one set of informants name their way of signing as *hands* or *mime* reminds us of the role that signing plays in the Yucatec village study by Johnson (1991) and in the Balinese village described by Branson, Miller, and Marsaja (1996). In those villages, sign language is used exclusively by deaf people as a form of communication with the other deaf villagers and with the great number of hearing villagers that sign, too. Johnson explains:

> [In the Yucatec village,] we do not observe any activities that could be labeled as exclusively (or even mostly) "deaf." Near the end of our visit, we gave a lunch party for all the deaf people and their extended families. To our knowledge, it was the first event in the village that was defined solely on the basis of deafness. . . . [D]eafness itself does not appear to have coalesced a strong ethnic group within the society of the village nor to have become politicized in the form of solidarity. (Johnson 1991)

This role of signing as solely a communicative tool among deaf people also explains the reasons given by some of our informants to explain the differences between their way of signing and that of the rest of Spain. Most of the informants refer to other varieties of signing by the name of the city where this variety is used (e.g., they say that the television program *En otras palabras* includes the signs from Madrid) or they answer with the peculiar sign glossed as SUYO (their own way).

The second idea that arises from analyzing the references to a distinct sign language is that the answers of the informants who consider their way of signing a language reflect a political decision, which in Bourdieu's (1992) terms, means that, for them, language has turned into an instrument of symbolic power.

> [A]lthough it is legitimate to treat social relations—even relations of domination—as symbolic interactions, that is, as relations of communication implying cognition and recognition, one must not forget that the relations of communication *par excellence*—linguistic exchanges—are also relations of symbolic power in which the power relations between speakers or their respective groups are actualized. (37)

The international movement for the political recognition of signed languages has occurred mainly in countries with developed democracies where deaf groups have been forced to organize themselves as ethnic and linguistic groups to defend their rights on equal terms with other minority groups. This description fits what we observed in the informants who identify their way of signing as a language. In societies like the Yucatec village described by Johnson (1991), where deaf people satisfy their economic and communicative needs within their family or neighborhood (they are farmers like everybody else in the village and they do not have problems of communication because a considerably large number of hearing can sign), considering deafness as a political phenomenon does not make any sense. Another interesting example of the different roles signing plays in rural and urban areas is explained by Jepson (1991), after research in different parts of India. Jepson also notices how these different communicative functions have important implications for the structural complexities of the signing codes.

Concerning the next question of the interview that asks about the level of understanding of foreign deaf people and other Spanish deaf people, most informants manifest difficulties in understanding the former but not the latter. From their answers, we can conclude that linguistic differences have not been a handicap for their mutual understanding. Thus, as Calvet (1998) proposes, we can deduce that the interrelation among them has always occurred despite their linguistic variations.

However, although mutual understanding has always been possible, one group believes that these differences are significant and that their form of signing deserves to be considered another language. When any of them uses the term LSC in this sense, replacing *signs, gestures,* or *hands,* he or she is not simply changing a word as when speakers or signers create new everyday words and substitute the old ones. On the contrary, he or she is activating a different "framework" (Goffman 1981), through which this signer indexes his or her alliance with the particular group that has taken a stand on a particular political decision with respect to the birth of a new language.

From the cognitive point of view, we could say that this lexical change is also associated with a specific mental image that guides this particular linguistic experience. Slobin (1991) explains this idea in the following way:

The expression of experience in linguistic terms constitutes "thinking for speaking"—a special form of thought that is mobilized for communication. . . . We encounter the contents of mind in a special way when they are being accessed for *use.* That is, the activity of thinking takes on a particular quality when it is used in the activity of speaking. In the evanescent time frame of constructing utterances in discourse one fits one's thoughts into available linguistic frames. (12)

In keeping with this opinion, shared by other researchers in ethnography of communication and interactional sociolinguistics, linguistic expressions not only are the mere reflection of reality outside us but also, at the same time, are constitutive of the reality that speakers or signers, as social actors, want to promote. Thus, when they name this external reality in a particular way, they also work for its constitution from that particular perspective.

The question now is whether or not it is possible to find an explanation for establishing such a clear-cut differentiation between LSC and LSE, especially when this decision has generated some ill feeling between the Catalan deaf community and deaf people in other parts of Spain and when almost every European country has only one sign language per state. A hypothesis that can explain this decision is that this decision could be a result of the influence of the nationalist Catalan movement. In the 1970s and 1980s, a strong movement emerged in Catalonia that fought for the public recognition of Catalan in every public sphere, as stated in the introduction of this work. This movement stands on a basic idea that stems from the 1960s, namely, the idea that, in Catalonia, there is a situation of conflict between two languages: a diglossic situation in which Catalan is dominated by Spanish. Hence, the only solution is to fight for the normalization of Catalan to bring about a change in the situation of Catalan (for a summary of these ideas and an alternative proposal see Boyer 1997).

Given this sociopolitical atmosphere that has dominated an important part of the intellectual and educational life in the 1970s and 1980s in Catalonia, there is hardly room for a position in favor of the defense of Spanish language and culture. This atmosphere could also explain the rejection on the part of the linguistic movement supported by the deaf community of the integration of their own signing variety within LSE. If, in addition, we take into account that the Catalan government—with nationalist sympathies and in power since the 1980s—has carried out a strong defense of Catalan culture (Catalan literature, music, etc.), we can propose that this political situation has contributed to emphasizing the differences with groups of deaf in other parts of Spain.

This phenomenon did not happen in other regions of Spain where a strong sense of identity and even a native language exist. For instance, in Valencia (where Valencian is spoken, a variety of Catalan), the level of lexical variation in signs in relation to the rest of the regions is also quite high (between 65 percent and 75 percent) according to Stephen and Dianne Parkhurst's scale (1998). However, the differences between the Valencia region and Catalonia lie in the fact that, in the former, the conflict of identity between what is Valencian and what is Spanish is an issue for only a minority segment of the population.

Finally, after we analyzed the differences observed in the videotaped conversations, we concluded that most of these differences concern lexical items. This conclusion confirms Stephen and Dianne Parkhurst's (1998) research. However, a detailed analysis of the lexical items shows that these differences are not at all uniform. That is, some forms differ only in some of their constitutive parameters but are similar in others, which indicates that those lexical items have a common history. We have also found cases where the same form is used, but with a different meaning (in some cases, a related meaning). Finally, we found that the average number of different signs is almost equal to the average number of related signs.

As we have suggested, this analysis of structural differences confirms the difference between signing in Catalonia and other varieties of signing. However this analysis reveals that linguistic variation among the two so-called languages can best be explained in terms of a continuum that encompasses diverse varieties, including variations among neighboring cities in Catalonia and the differences observed in signs used in other cities outside Catalonia as some of our informants have explicitly suggested.

The focus on only one city implies that our research has certain limitations because it does not allow us to draw any further conclusions about the linguistic differences between LSE and LSC. However, our research reveals that these differences may be gradual and not as discrete as one set of our informants maintain.

At the same time, the results of our research allow us to suggest some guidelines that may be useful for people involved in the standardization of sign language in Catalonia. First, we think that any intervention in language can come about only after a thorough linguistic and sociolinguistic study of the whole territory of Catalonia and the surrounding area. As Rodríguez Yáñez (1997) states in his proposal for a bilingual situation in Galicia, the conflict between languages may exist only in elite intellectual spheres, and the empirical reality may reveal other differences that must be taken into account (194, 196).[12]

12. For example, as far as the situation in Galicia is concerned, the most recent sociolinguistic studies confirm social differences between the rural environment (primarily speakers of Galician or of varieties midway between Galician and Spanish) and the urban context (primarily speakers of Spanish).

In addition, any intervention in sign language should be made only after a debate has taken place among all the users and once a broad consensus has been reached. If we consider this intervention a question of planned intervention in a language, Calvet's (1998) distinction between in vivo and in vitro intervention could be useful. The first type of intervention concerns the spontaneous management that arises and comes from specific social practices, and the latter refers to the intervention directed by empowered groups (in the case of a national language, the government itself).

Our empirical data show that the difference between signing in Catalonia and the rest of Spain is considered by our informants to be based on their own way of signing, that is, a movement that has arisen in vivo through particular communicative practices over the years. However, the differences in the names used to refer to signing that are noted by one group (who use the term LSC) seem to arise from a more planned linguistic intervention (that is, in vitro). And, as Calvet himself has stated on many occasions (recently, see Calvet 2000), with in vitro intervention, tensions can arise between the practices of the linguistic users and the decisions of the politicians, tensions that can even lead to the failure of standardization: "Lorsque les solutions avancées *in vitro* vont dans le sens des pratiques *in vivo,* les opérations réussissent en général. Les problèmes commencent lorsque les locuteurs ne veulent pas des décisions prises par les politiques, et l'on va alors les plus souvent à l'échec" (184).[13] In these cases, only more democratic and less imperative solutions can lead to a resolution of the conflict (189).

Finally, we think that any decision should be long-term and should consider the complexity of the trilingual education programs envisioned for the future if the bilingual method (sign language and oral language) is adopted. We must add to these considerations the problems that could arise if a clear-cut distinction is made between LSC and LSE, taking into account any possible harm that this distinction may cause with respect to the education of deaf people in general. Clearly, we must respect the present differences in the two approaches to signing; however, we wonder whether it makes any sense to create different signs to be used in the technical and scientific material incorporated into the curriculum to reflect dif-

---

13. In English, the quote is "When the solutions elaborated *in vitro* derive from practice *in vivo,* the operation is usually a success. The problems arise when speakers do not accept the decisions taken by politicians, in which case the operation sometimes fails."

ferences between signing in Catalonia and signing in the rest of the country.[14] Perhaps, a commission representing the different interests of the two sectors that are involved in planning the relevant social and educational programs could resolve this conflict in such a way that the goal of educational simplicity is served.

REFERENCES

Aracil, Li. V., 1966. Bilingulism as myth. *Cahiers de L' IRCE,* 4, Centre Universitaire de Perpignan, France.

Aramburo, A. J. 1989. Sociolinguistic aspects of the black deaf community. In *Sociolinguistics of the deaf community,* ed. C. Lucas, 103–19. San Diego, Calif.: Academic Press.

Bellés, R. M., P. Cedillo, J. González de Ibarra, and E. Molins. 2000. The education of deaf children in Barcelona. In *Bilingualism and identity in deaf communities,* ed. M. Metzger, 95–113. Sociolinguistics in Deaf Communities Series, vol. 6. Washington, D.C.: Gallaudet University Press.

Boix, E., and J. Vila. 1998. *Sociolingüística Catalana.* Barcelona: Ariel.

Bourdieu, P. 1992. *Language and symbolic power.* Oxford: Polity Press.

Boyer, H. 1997. Conflic d'usages, conflic d'images. In *Plurilinguisme: 'Contact' ou 'conflict' de langues?,* ed. H. Boyer, 9–35. Paris: L'Harmattan.

Branson, J., D. Miller, and I. G. Marsaja. 1996. Everyone here speaks sign language, too: A deaf village in Bali, Indonesia. In *Multicultural aspects of sociolinguistics in deaf communities,* ed. C. Lucas, 39–57. Sociolinguistics in Deaf Communities Series, vol. 2. Washington, D.C.: Gallaudet University Press.

Burns, S. E. 1998. Irish Sign Language: Ireland's second minority language. In *Pinky extension and eye gaze: Language use in deaf communities,* ed. C. Lucas, 233–73. Sociolinguistics in Deaf Communities Series, vol. 4. Washington, D.C.: Gallaudet University Press.

Calvet, L.-J. 1998. *A (socio)linguistica.* Santiago de Compostela, Spain: Laiovento.

———. 2000. Langues et développement: Agir sur les représentations? *Estudios de Sociolingüística* 1 (1): 183–90.

Cheng, L. L. 2000. Deafness: An Asian/Pacific perspective. In *Deaf plus: A multicultural perspective,* ed. K. Christensen and G. Delgado, 59–92. San Diego, Calif.: DawnSignPress.

14. Neither LSC nor LSE have a tradition of forming new signs based on dactylology as in ASL.

Christensen, K., and G. Delgado. 2000. *Deaf plus: A multicultural perspective.* San Diego, Calif.: DawnSignPress.

Delgado, G. L., ed. 1984. *The Hispanic deaf: Issues and challenges for bilingual special education.* Washington, D.C.: Gallaudet College Press.

Delgado, G. L. 2000 How are we going? In *Deaf plus: A multicultural perspective,* ed. K. Christensen and G. Delgado, 41–58. San Diego, Calif.: DawnSignPress.

Direcció General de Política Lingüística. 1996. *El coneixement del Català.* Barcelona: Generalitat de Catalunya.

Duranti, A. 1994. *From grammar to politics: Linguistic anthropology in a western Samoan village.* Los Angeles: University of California Press.

Fasold, R. 1987. *The sociolinguistics of society.* Oxford: Blackwell.

Fernández Soneira, A. 2000. El número y la cuantificación en la lengua de Señas Española. Master's thesis, University of Vigo, Spain.

Fourestier, S. 2002. Verbos de movimiento y locación en la LSC: Un estudio sobre verbos complejos en la lengua de Signos Catalana. *Lynx.* Working paper, University of Valencia, Spain.

Gerner de García, B. 1995. Communication and language use in Spanish-speaking families with deaf children. In *Sociolinguistics in deaf communities,* ed. C. Lucas, 221–52. The Sociolinguistics in Deaf Communities Series, vol. 1. Washington, D.C.: Gallaudet University Press.

Goffman, E. 1981. *Forms of talk.* Philadelphia: University of Pennsylvania Press.

Grimes, J. E. 1995. *Language survey reference guide.* Dallas: Summer Institute of Linguistics.

Grosjean, F. 1982. *Life with two languages.* Cambridge, Mass.: Harvard University Press.

Gumperz, J. J. 1982a. *Discourse strategies.* Cambridge: Cambridge University Press.

———. 1982b. *Language and social identity.* Cambridge: Cambridge University Press.

Hansen, B. 2002. Bilingualism and the impact of sign language research on deaf education. In *The study of signed languages,* ed. David F. Armstrong, Michael A. Karchmer, and John Vickrey Van Cleve. Washington, D.C.: Gallaudet University Press.

Jepson, J. 1991. Urban and rural sign language in India. *Language in Society* 20: 37–57.

Johnson, R. E. 1991. Sign language, culture, and community in a traditional Yucatec Maya village. *Sign Language Studies* 73 (CD-ROM version).

Johnson, R. E., and C. Erting. 1989. Ethnicity and socialization in a classroom for deaf children. In *Sociolinguistics of the deaf community,* ed. C. Lucas, 41–83. San Diego, Calif.: Academic Press.

Johnston, T. 1998. *Signs of Australia: A new dictionary of Auslan.* New South Wales, Australia: North Rocks Press.

Kannapell, B. 1989. An examination of deaf college students' attitudes toward ASL and English. In *Sociolinguistics of the deaf community,* ed. C. Lucas, 191–210. San Diego, Calif.: Academic Press.

———. 1993. *Language choice—Identity choice.* Burtonsville, Md.: Linstok Press Dissertation Series.

Labov, W. 1972. *Sociolinguistic patterns.* Philadelphia: University of Pennsylvania Press.

Lambert, W. E., and G. R. Tucker. 1972. *Bilingual education of children: The St. Lambert experiment.* Rowley, Mass.: Newbury House.

Lerman, A. 1984. Survey of Hispanic hearing-impaired students and their families in New York City. In *The Hispanic deaf: Issues and challenges for bilingual special education,* ed. G. L. Delgado, 38–56. Washington, D.C.: Gallaudet College Press.

Lucas, C., and C. Valli. 1989. Language contact in the American deaf community. In *Sociolinguistics of the deaf community,* ed. C. Lucas, 11–40. San Diego: Calif.: Academic Press.

———. 1992. *Language contact in the American deaf community.* New York: Academic Press.

Martínez Sánchez, F., et al. 2000. *Apuntes de lingüística de la lengua de Signos Española.* Madrid: Confederación Nacional de Sordos Españoles (CNSE).

Oviedo, A. 1996. Bilingual deaf education in Venezuela: Linguistics comments on the current situation. In *Multicultural aspects of sociolinguistics in deaf communities,* ed. C. Lucas, 61–79. Sociolinguistics in Deaf Communities Series, vol. 2. Washington, D.C.: Gallaudet University Press.

Padden, C. 1989. The deaf community and the culture of deaf people. In *American deaf culture. An anthology,* ed. S. Wilcox, 1–16. Burtonsville, Md.: Linstok Press.

Parkhurst, S., and D. Parkhurst. 1998. La variación en las lenguas de signos. *Revista Española de Lingüística de las Lenguas de Signos* 1: 29–55.

Pinedo Peydró, F. J. 2000. *Diccionario de la lengua de Signos Española.* Madrid: Confederación Nacional de Sordos Españoles (CNSE).

Plann, S. 1997. *A silent minority: Deaf education in Spain, 1550–1835.* Berkeley: University of California.

Pradilla, M. A. 2001. The Catalan-speaking communities. In *Multilingualism in Spain,* ed. M. T. Turell, 58–90. Clevedon, U.K.: Multilingual Matters.

Pujolar, J. 2001. *Gender, heteroglossia and power: A sociolinguistic study of youth culture.* Berlin: Mouton de Gruyter.

Ramsey, C. 1997. *Deaf children in public schools: Placement, context, and consequences.* Washington, D.C.: Gallaudet University Press.

———. 2000. On the border: Cultures, families, and schooling in a transnational region. In *Deaf plus: A multicultural perspective,* ed. K. Christensen and G. Delgado, 121–47. San Diego, Calif: DawnSignPress.

Rodríguez González, M. A. 1992. *Lenguaje de signos.* Madrid: Confederación Nacional de Sordos Españoles/Organización Nacional de Ciegos Españoles.

Rodríguez Yáñez, X. P. 1997. Aléas theoriques et méthodologiques dans l'etude du bilinguisme: Le cas de la Galice. In *Plurilinguisme: "Contact" ou "conflict" de langues?,* ed. H. Boyer 191–254. Paris: L'Harmattan.

Slobin, D. 1991. Learning to think for speaking: Native language, cognition, and rhetorical style. *Pragmatics* 1 (1): 7–25.

Ward Trotter, J. 1989. An examination of language attitudes of teachers of the deaf. In *Sociolinguistics of the deaf community,* ed. C. Lucas, 211–28. San Diego, Calif.: Academic Press.

Wilcox, S., ed. 1989. *American deaf culture: An anthology.* Burtonsville, Md.: Linstok Press.

Questionnaire Used with Casal and Cerecusor Subjects

LANGUAGE ATTITUDES TEST

Test number:
Interviewer:
Date:
Place:

PART I: PERSONAL ASPECTS

1. Age:
2. Female/male?
3. Place of birth:
4. Where do you live now?
5. Are you married, separated, single?   To deaf/hearing?
6. Have you got any children?   How many?   Deaf/hearing?
7. Do you study?

> Yes   What do you study?
> Where?

8. Have you got a job?

> Yes   What's your job?
> No   Have you had a job before?
> What was your work?

9. The cause of your deafness is:

a. From birth	Yes	Age	Level of loss:
b. From accident	Yes	Age:	Level of loss:
c. From sickness	Yes	Age:	Level of loss:
d. Other causes	Yes	Age:	Level of loss:

10. Have you got any deaf relatives?   Yes   How many?   Who are they?
11. Which relatives do you use signs with?

PART 2: EDUCATIONAL ASPECTS

1. What school did you study at? For how long?
2. Did you go to Secondary school? Professional? How long?
3. Did you go to University? Which one? For how long?
4. Did you use to sign at school, the Secondary school or University?
5. Which were your favourite subjects?
6. Were signs used in any of the subjects?

PART 3: COMMUNICATIVE ASPECTS

1. How do you usually communicate?
2. How do you usually communicate with a hearing person?
3. If you use spoken language, is it Spanish or Catalan?
4. Are the signs you use with a deaf person different to the ones you use with a hearing person?

    Why?
    Why do you think they are different?

5. Do you use signs with:

    a. relatives
    b. friends
    c. at the association/club
    d. at work
    e. others?

6. Do you attend conferences, courses, or meetings?
7. Do you usually watch TV? Signed programs? Captioned programs?
8. Are the signs on TV different?

    What is the difference?

9. Have you been in contact with deaf from other areas in Spain? Which areas?

    Are the signs different? How different?
    Do you understand each other? Why?

10. Have you been in contact with deaf people from abroad? Which areas?

   Are the signs different?   How different?
   Do you understand one another?   Why?

11. Do you use interpreting services?

   One to one services?   Conferences?   Courses?

12. When you talk to an interpreter, do you sign differently?
13. Is is difficult to understand interpreters?

VIDEO:

Tell us:

1. Where do you think the people appearing on the video are from?
2. Do you understand what they are saying?

APPENDIX B

Characteristics of Interviewed Individuals

Sex	Age	Birthplace	Hearing Loss	Marital Status	Couple	Children	Deaf/ Hearing	Deaf Family Members	Association Membership	School
Male	35	Barcelona	2 1/2 years	Married	Deaf	1	Hearing	none	Casal	Centro Médico de Audición y Lenguaje
Female	36	Barcelona	1 year	Married	Deaf	2	Hearing	Mother, cousins, uncles	Casal	Centro Médico de Audición y Lenguaje
Female	46	Barcelona	Birth	Married	Deaf	3	Both	Brother	Casal	Centro Municipal Fonoaudiológico
Male	19	Barcelona	Birth	Single	—	—	—	Parents, brother, uncle	Casal	Mainstream
Female	70	Madrid	Birth	Married	Deaf	1	Hearing	Parents, uncle	Casal	Purísima Barcelona
Female	16	Barcelona	2 years	—	—	—	—	None	Casal	Mainstream
Male	37	Barcelona	7 years	—	—	—	—	Brother	Casal	Mainstream
Female	83	Tarragona	Birth	Married	Deaf	2	Hearing	None	Casal	Centro Municipal Fonoaudiológico
Female	84	Almería	8 years	Widow	Deaf	4	Hearing	None	Casal	Centro Municipal Fonoaudiológico
Female	48	Jaén	4 months	Married	Deaf	2	Hearing	None	Casal	Colegio de Sordomudos de Madrid
Female	36	Barcelona	3 months	Married	Hearing	—	—	None	Casal	Special school
Male	35	Barcelona	2 years	Married	Deaf	2	Hearing	None	Casal	Escuela Municipal
Male	53	Lleida	1 year	Married	Deaf	1	Hearing	None	Casal	Centro Municipal Fonoaudiológico
Female	35	Córdoba	18 months	Married	Deaf	—	—	Cousin	Casal	Centro Municipal Fonoaudiológico
Female	32	Barcelona	1 year	Married	Deaf	1	Hearing	None	Casal	Centro Municipal Fonoaudiológico
Female	26	Barcelona	Birth	—	—	—	—	None	Casal	Mainstream

Sex	Age	City	Onset	Marital status	Deaf	No.	Parents	Relatives		Education / Association
Male	33	Seu d'Urgell	6 months	Married	Deaf	—	—	None	Cerecusor	Centro Médico de Audición y Lenguaje
Male	34	Barcelona	3 years	Married	Deaf	1	Deaf	None	Cerecusor	Mainstream
Male	17	Barcelona	Birth	—	—	—	—	Brother	Cerecusor	Josep Pla—special school
Male	17	Barcelona	Birth	—	—	—	—	Parents, brothers	Cerecusor	Purísima, CRAS, Consell de Cent
Male	28	Barcelona	Birth	—	—	—	—	Brother	Cerecusor	Centro Médico de Audición y Lenguaje and mainstream
Male	31	Barcelona	Birth	Single	—	—	—	Sister, cousin	Cerecusor	Mainstream
Female	30	Almería	Birth	Divorced	Deaf	3	Both	None	Cerecusor	Purísima Granada
Female	43	Palencia	9 months	Married	Deaf	3	Hearing	None	Cerecusor	Purísima Madrid and Barcelona
Male	38	Barcelona	2 years	Married	Deaf	2	Hearing	Mother, brothers	Cerecusor	Purísima
Male	70	Torelló	1 year	Divorced	Deaf	1	Deaf	Child	Cerecusor	Purísima
Male	69	Barcelona	Birth	Divorced	Deaf	1	Hearing	None	Cerecusor	Laboratorio de la Palabra, Centro Municipal Fonoaudiológico, Purísima
Male	31	Barcelona	Birth	Married	Deaf	1	Hearing	None	Cerecusor	Mainstream
Male	85	Barcelona	Birth	Married	Deaf	1	Deaf	Parents, uncles, children, cousins	Cerecusor	Purísima, Istituto Catalan del Sordo
Male	72	Lloret de Mar	Birth	Widow	Deaf	1	Deaf	Child	Cerecusor	Purísima
Female	55	Subirats	1 year	Married	Deaf	3	Hearing	None	Cerecusor	Mainstream
Male	23	Sabadell	12 years	Single	—	—	—	Parents	Cerecusor	Mainstream
Male	20	Barcelona	Birth	Single	—	—	—	Parents	Cerecusor	Graphic Design
Female	82	Tarragona	1 year	Married	Deaf	1	Deaf	Child	Cerecusor	Purísima

Index

transcription conventions, 50
transliterating, defined, 27
Larrue, J., 83
Latin America and trilingualism of deaf people, 109
Lexicalized fingerspelling, 6, 20
Liddell, S., 4, 14, 35, 41, 62
Linguistics of Visual English (LOVE), 28, 30
Location, 33, 41–42
LSC. *See* Catalan Sign Language
LSE. *See* Spanish Sign Language
Lucas, C., 10, 31, 32, 36, 39, 41, 42, 45, 113

Mainstreaming in Barcelona, 123, 126, 140–41
Male vs. female. *See* Gender differences, and usage of ASL
Malloy, C., 8
Mansfield, D., 8
Manual channel, 33, 39–42
  grammatical categories of signs, 39
  salient ASL features, 39–42
Manually coded English (MCE), 30–31, 44, 46
Marsaja, G., 142
Masks in research, 119–20
Mayan deaf community and trilingualism, 109
MCE. *See* Manually coded English
McMurtrie, J., 7–8
Mental spaces, 54–56
  base space, 54–55, 59
Metaphor, 54
Metzger, M., 59, 62, 73, 93–94, 98, 101
Milan Conference (1880), 74
Miller, D., 142
Mixed meetings of Deaf signers and hearing nonsigners, 73–74, 77–78, 84–98. *See also* Turntaking mechanisms in Flanders
Mouth channel

ASL and English features found in, 32–33, 37–39
  full English mouthing, 33, 37
    without sign support, 39, 45
  mouthing co-occurring with sign support, 37–39, 44
  mouthing in isolation, 43–44
Movements, 4–5, 33

National Confederation of the Deaf in Spain, 113
NAVEKADOS, 75
The Neighbor (movie), 44
Netherlands, Sign Language of (SLN), 32
Nouns and citation form in ASL fingerspelling, 18
Nowell, E., 7, 8

Observer's Paradox, 9–10
Oviedo, A., 126

Padden, C., 5, 6, 28, 33, 44
Palm orientation, 33
Parkhurst, S. & D., 114, 115, 144, 145
Pidgin Signed English (PSE), 28, 30, 31–32
  ASL features occurring in, 31
  codeswitching, 34
  English features occurring in, 31
  examples of English features in, 36
  use by individuals bilingual in ASL and English, 31
  vs. MCEs, 31
Plann, S., 124

Real Space, 55, 59
Referents, establishment and identification of, 41, 42
Registry of Interpreters for the Deaf, Inc. (RID), 29
  Certificate of Transliteration, 28
  evaluation system, 29
Reiteration and gender differences in use of, 8

in mixed meetings with sign language interpreters, 84–92, 99–101

Valencia, Spain, 114, 115, 144–45
Valli, C., 10, 31, 32, 36, 39, 41, 42, 45, 113
VARBRUL program and analysis fingerspelling, 13–17, 18–20
step-up and step-down procedure, 15, 16, 18
Variation in ASL fingerspelling, 3–23
ASL fingerspelling, 4–6
binomial variable rule analysis results, 15, 19
citation form, defined, 3
final study, 17–21
data, 9–11
discussion, 20–21
results, 18–20
fingerspelled sign preceding another fingerspelled sign, 14, 15, 16, 18–20
fingerspelled word vs. fingerspelled sign in pilot study, 12
gender differences. *See* Gender differences, and usage of ASL
grammatical function as factor, 16, 18, 21
incompletely articulated or missing letters, 6
lexicalized fingerspelling, 6, 20
noncitation form

difficulty in understanding, 3, 9, 13, 21
influential factors in production of, 15
noncitation form and difficulty in understanding, 3, 9, 13
orientation as factor, 14, 16
phonological differences in ASL signing, 8–9, 21
pilot study, 11–17
coding, 11–14
data, 9–11
discussion, 16–17
fingerspelled word vs. fingerspelled sign, 12
results, 14–15
Venezuela and deaf education, 126
Verbs and citation form in ASL fingerspelling, 18, 20
Vila, J., 110

Walloon, 75–76
Ward Trotter, J., 120
Wiener, M., 79
Wilcox, S., 6
Winston, E., 59
Women vs. men. *See* Gender differences, and usage of ASL
Wulf, A., 8

Yãnez, Rodríguez, 145